WITHDRAWN

Blind Man on a Freeway

The Community College Administrator

william moore, jr.

BLIND MAN ON A FREEWAY

 Jossey-Bass Inc., Publishers

San Francisco · Washington · London · 1971

BLIND MAN ON A FREEWAY
The Community College Administrator
by William Moore, Jr.

Published in Great Britain by
Jossey-Bass, Inc., Publishers
St. George's House
44 Hatton Garden, London E.C.1

Library of Congress Catalogue Card Number LC 72-168858

International Standard Book Number ISBN 0-87589-106-3

Manufactured in the United States of America

JACKET DESIGN BY WILLI BAUM

FIRST EDITION

Code 7132

The Jossey-Bass
Series in Higher Education

JOHN E. ROUECHE

Consulting Editor, Community and Junior Colleges

To Rosetta

Preface

When I originally titled this book *Blind Man on a Freeway,* a noted educator advised against it: "I really believe you should not title the book *Blind Man on a Freeway.* It is a bit too flippant and will not set quite right with the average administrator. You know yourself that the average academic has no sense of humor and takes himself very seriously. You need a somewhat more staid title." Yet, the administrator who is without a sense of humor is headed for what we in the field have come to call ulcer gulch. There is little reason to hassle about what a volume is called. The title of a book is but advance notice of its content. There are important reasons for writing it. The following are my reasons.

Educators no longer tell the truth. They do not even tell believable lies. They obscure facts with inaccurate research and with jargon that few people understand. This problem of credibility is most discernible in the area of higher education administration.

Library shelves already groan under the weight of books on college administration. There are simply too many, and it is difficult to find any variation in their content. Most, if not all, of these publications serve as little more than theoretical handbooks in required graduate courses leading to an advanced degree or job certification for principals and superintendents. Their content provides little practical information to the man who is entering higher education administration. And, in spite of a proliferation of these books, one does not find one addressed to the community college administrator.

What I am concerned with throughout *Blind Man on a Freeway* is that specific administrator and the problems of his institution as they emerged during the 1960s. I have left the philosophy, the organizational structure, the leadership and management theories (the coordination of/role of/function of/control of/and direction of), and the academic solutions and discussions to my predecessors. They apparently have the tolerance and persistence to deal with speculation. While my colleagues have been prolific in their hypotheses and their publication credits are enviable, they have not concerned themselves with the problems of the two-year college administrator either in theory or in practice.

It will be at once apparent to the reader of *Blind Man on a Freeway* that I contend that this administrator is poorly trained for his job; his administrative know-how is two decades behind the crucial problems and issues facing two-year colleges. I suggest that the current graduate school intern programs for administrators are nothing more than extended field trips, characterized by assigning the administrative trainee to do projects, write term papers, read and report on bibliographies, complete case studies, and perform the other well known academic minutiae prescribed by scholars for practitioners. These scholars maintain that those who want to become administrators must qualify by doing graduate work; and all who expect to become chief administrators must hold Ph.D.s. But the compulsion of fulfilling these two requirements does not render many of their graduates fit for administrative duty in the community college. The scholars create other criteria that even their predecessors refused to entertain, and they defend the shibboleths that contemporary college managers reject. They continue to evolve curricula out of the womb of the library stacks.

Blind Man on a Freeway notes that the community college

Preface

administrator's role and function are the least defined of those for any educational administrator. There are, to be sure, varying perceptions of what the community college administrator is or appears to be. In their lounge, I heard a group of faculty describe an administrator as reluctant, permissive, inaccessible, an incompetent ass, unresponsive, ineffectual, vacillating, and gutless. Later, in the dining hall, I heard him described as capable, directive, aggressive, flexible, strong-willed, "his own man," effective, and blunt. This schizophrenic, by another name, is an administrator. Only in a community college do the students, faculty, classified personnel, and community members get close enough to the administrator to make these judgments. One thing is certain: among this constituency, one cannot expect consensus.

In *Blind Man on a Freeway* I identify several of the new groups with whom the administrator in the community college must interact and some of the problems, behaviors, and attitudes he can expect to encounter. I give special attention to militant and minority groups; explore some of the problems in the collective bargaining process; and discuss the educationally disadvantaged students enrolled in the two-year college.

My effort is to call attention to the need for establishing relevant professional education for administrators who must deal with this new community college constituency. Valid principles which permit us to interpret and control the administrator's education process are needed. At present, we continue to use training programs based on tradition, knowledge salvaged from the elementary and secondary school principalship, personal experience, and on-the-job training. Professors in administrator training institutions are satisfied to proceed on the basis of the experience of the past rather than the needs of the present and future. New ideas can appear threatening to the academician who considers himself secure in time-tested methods. And, to be sure, not all the old techniques are bad. But the administrative trainee has a right to expect the best, most up-to-date training possible. To provide him with anything less makes those who train him and the institutions which award him his degree academic frauds.

Preface

Throughout this volume, I have substituted pseudonyms for the exact names of certain people and community colleges—to protect the guilty.

No author writes a book alone. Many people touch a volume before it reaches fruition. Some have great impact on it. Some don't. I should like to acknowledge the assistance I received from Ann K. Pruitt, who, in her spare time, worked as secretary, typist, proofreader, and critic to complete the manuscript.

This book is for Rosetta, who has given up "the impossible dream" of getting a busy administrator home to dinner on time.

Columbus, Ohio
September 1971

WILLIAM MOORE, JR.

Contents

Contents

Blind Man on a Freeway

The Community College Administrator

It is not the rhetoric and villainies of war, poverty, crime, drugs, violence, racism, and their harvest of backlash, law and order, and repression; it is not the report that God is dead, the suppression of academic freedom, or even truth that educators fear. It is *change*.

WILLIAM MOORE, JR.
Excerpt from a speech
University of Washington
February 13, 1970

Administrators as Blind Men

It is no secret! The community college needs a well trained new breed of administrative leadership. This leadership must be strong, reflective, decisive, honest, and flexible because it cannot—and will not—be insulated from the dilemmas of action. This leadership must be manifest in men who have the capacity to understand and appraise the performance and activities of others and to recommend sound courses of action. These leaders must not vacillate in their decisions regardless of pressures and stresses. Because of these stresses, pressures, frustrations, and conflicts of the job, the new community college leader cannot expect to earn his pension on one assignment. His calling card may well include the following admonition: Have resume—will travel. Yet, leaders cannot avoid controversy. Dispute is the midwife of academic freedom and social change; and the community college administrator must be able to accept dissent as routine.

1

In addition he must be sensitive to social issues which defy simple explanation; he must understand that these issues are a definite part of his institution and community. Among the implications for him is that even though he is an academician, he must rediscover the working man. The forces underlying a comprehensive community college require him to be sophisticated in knowledge and skill but unpretentious in his interaction with the community he serves. He must also have a tolerance for country estates, rat-infested slum dwellings, and dirty houses with crawling cockroaches. These are the homes that send him his students. Finally, in an environment symbolized by the anonymous IBM card, he can expect to encounter the seething and simmering discontent of students and to have to negotiate with faculty. Most of all, the community college needs new administrators who know what they are doing in all these areas. Too many get paid for doing a job they cannot do. Every taxpayer should demand that these welfare payments stop.

On the other hand, the taxpayer and the academic community need to understand and appreciate the community college administrator and his problems. The public has a distorted image of the administrator. Citizens tend to think of him as being the boss—an executive who spends his time in sophisticated circles and in making broad, unilateral educational decisions. The academic community knows better. In fact, the chief complaint of deans is that they do not have authority to accompany their responsibilities. To paraphrase Ingraham and King (1968, p. 3), higher education has two goals for administrators: overwork them; turn them into vassals. It achieves the first objective but usually fails to completely accomplish the second one. Many administrators quit before they become complete handymen. Yet, in spite of their work loads, "they remain men of vigor and intelligence. They do not lose their zest for life or their devotion to education. Generally, they grow in wisdom, often in humor, sometimes in wit." Some "grow" ulcers. They are much more open to reform in the educational program than are the faculty (Taylor, 1971, p. 59). And, unlike other members of the college community, they do not complain about their salaries when they know the financial problems of the institution (Ingraham and King, 1968, p. 16).

Before we further explore the problems and opportunities or virtues of the community college administrator, a definition of the term *administrator* is appropriate. In this volume it means those professionals who have supervisory or managerial control over other employees. Typical job titles included in this category are president or vice-president, dean, assistant dean, associate dean, assistant department chairman, division chairman, department chairman, supervisor, director, coordinator, and administrative assistant.

A new Ph.D. who comes to the two-year institution with his degree in higher education administration or in guidance and counseling or the professor of administration who leaves academe for the real world walks into an institution pocked and pitted with ineffective instruction in some fundamental skill areas (Gleazer, 1968; Moore, 1970a); with power struggles among its different constituencies (Keeton, 1971); and with problems of identity. It is an institution where too many teachers continue to use outmoded and traditional methods (Kelley and Wilbur, 1970; Yegge, 1968; Taylor, 1969, 1971); where little or no research and publication is done (Schoonmaker, 1971, p. 81); where the integrity of programs is questionable (Spencer, 1971, p. 20); where there appears to be no room for administrative leadership because the traditional professorial view of academic democracy is that "the faculty decides policy in town-meeting style and administrators are their emasculated servants" (Livingston, 1968, p. 188); and where some administrators still believe in the monarchy for themselves. It is an institution making increasing appeals to the federal government to replace the deteriorating financial support at the local level with federal funds (Mensel, 1971, p. 11); and one with the ever present potential for racial conflicts (Lombardi, 1969). The institution, though young, is becoming so constipated with the traditions inherited from the university and the common school that little change can occur. Several authors have noted this sluggishness to change in the community college (Medsker, 1960; Roueche, 1970; Jennings, 1970; Moore, 1970a). Placed in this situation, the new two-

3

year college administrator is like a blind man on a freeway. His degree is little more than a white cane. He cannot depend on what he has learned to get him to his destination safely and with dispatch. Too much of what he has to do depends upon skills he has yet to master and the behavior of others. He has spent most of his academic training dealing with philosophical constructs and performing classroom exercises. Virtually none of this training is in solving practical problems in the community college. So during his first one or two years in the institution, he gets his training on the job. He receives his instruction from other people—mainly from secretaries, clerks, and students—who earn his salary for him and who eventually teach him what he is supposed to know, what he is supposed to do, how, and why. He learns from his mistakes, many of which are unnecessary. Such trial-and-error learning is expensive, inefficient, unpredictable, and sometimes counterproductive. The men who are lucky enough to have had some experience teaching or working as administrators prior to earning an advanced degree are better candidates for administrative positions in open-door colleges. But even they have had sterile experiences if they have not spent some time in inner city or rural institutions. The problems among the students enrolled in these institutions are if not more severe certainly much more sensational than are those found in the suburban colleges and in proprietary schools.

The promise of effective administration in the community college was greater in the mid-1960s than it is now. Richardson (1970), a graduate of the W. K. Kellogg Junior College Leadership Program and a coauthor of *The Two-Year College: A Social Synthesis,* has written:

There are a number of trends which promise to stimulate significant changes in the two-year college. First the development of the W. K. Kellogg Junior College Leadership Program in ten major universities has stimulated the professional education of larger numbers of individuals for administrative posts in two-year colleges. The impact of this foundation support will be felt within the next few years when these well trained leaders begin to fill top administrative posts in colleges in the various states, universities, and state departments of education. Perhaps of equal importance is the encouragement of the scholarly study of two-year colleges by professors of educational administration and graduate students. The fruits of this research are beginning to appear in publications and, hopefully, will encourage innovations and improvements in college administrative practices.

Five years later, after experience as a dean and as a community college president, he writes:

> *The question can legitimately be raised as to whether a science of administration may be said to exist with respect to two-year colleges. I would tend to feel from personal observation that current practice represents a hodgepodge of ideas garnered from business, secondary schools, and four-year universities without the benefit of much analysis as to how well these ideas relate to the kinds of problems currently being encountered by the administrative organizations of two-year colleges.*

The difficulties of administration in the community college today exceed the hypothetical problems solved in graduate school. Yet, graduate professors in higher education continue to ram these curricula and experiences down the throats of their students in administration. This observation is not a case against theory. Some theory is obviously necessary. Rather, it is the plea that the theoreticians also be aware of practical applications. It is not at all unusual to find professors teaching courses on the community college who have never been in a community college and who cannot describe what it is or what it does. In 1969 an administrative intern assigned to Forest Park Community College in St. Louis polled 102 four-year colleges and universities offering one or more courses in community college education. The purpose of the survey was to determine whether the professors teaching the courses had any community college teaching experience. Of the 131 professors identified, only seven had two-year college experience; 81 had never been inside a community college (Scruggs, 1969). In one mid-eastern university, I was invited to visit a seminar on community college administration. The teacher was a professor in the higher education administration department. All his students were Ph.D. candidates. The following (as I recall) is the dialogue in one particular exchange between the teacher and one of his seminarians:

"Dr. X, what would be your way of funding an academic program in a comprehensive community college? On the basis of program? Or on the basis of F.T.E.s? And if you used F.T.E.s, should you weight them in vocational areas?"

"What are F.T.E.s?"

"Sir?"

"What are F.T.E.s?"

"Oh, ah, full-time equivalent students."

"I have never heard of that. Is it new? This is something that the whole class would be interested in. Could I prevail upon you to enlighten us."

The student "volunteered." It was difficult for him to hide his embarrassment since he knew that most if not all the other students in the class already knew what he was explaining to them. Some knew because they worked in community colleges; some knew from their reading; others knew from conversations; and still others knew because the information is as common as breathing in two-year college circles. The average freshman student in the community college can explain the meaning of F.T.E.s. For the professor to ask what they were was tantamount to a doctor's asking, "What is blood, and is it new?"

I sat in this seminar for two hours, and the professor thoroughly convinced me that he knew virtually nothing about community colleges, how they operate, or what they do. After the class, I had my appraisal confirmed. The students, like many graduate students, were aware of their teacher's lack of competence and expertise in the area of community college administration. But even they were shocked to discover that he did not know about something as fundamental as F.T.E.s. Graduate students learned long ago that one serves his time and does not disturb the waters. They know that it is deadly for them to challenge the professor (Van den Berghe, 1970) or to spend their time doing creative work (Schoon-maker, 1971).

Many of the scholars who work in administrator-training institutions cannot write a job description for and cannot define the role of the administrators they train; and they cannot explain the essential differences between the administrative function in the four-year college or university and that function in the community college. To be sure, they do overlap. They are also quite different. It is useful for us in this chapter to explore the functions and prob-lems of the community college administrator and to compare them with those of his counterparts in elementary and high schools and in four-year institutions. In this way we can obtain some perspective on the dilemmas community college administrators face and perhaps obtain also some insight into how to resolve them. In later chapters I present my suggestions for solutions and also return to the problem of inadequate training.

Blocker and others (1965) describe the ways in which two-year college presidents (public and private) spend their time. (Private junior colleges are university prototypes.) In general, public college presidents spend more time than do private college presidents in meeting with members of the board, in coordination with other educational programs and institutions, in recruiting and selecting faculty, and in relations with the state legislature and state agencies. Private college presidents spend more time than public college presidents in public relations, in coordination with other community programs and organizations, in fund-raising, and in student programs and problems. Both presidents spend about equal amounts of time in general administration and in dealing with educational organizations.

The community college president however now finds himself and his college taking on more social, instrumental, and residual functions than those listed by Blocker. A social function is self-explanatory. An instrumental function is one that the college is not required to offer but that will help the student adjust to the college and learning environment. Providing free tutoring services and

7

scholarships are examples. A residual function is one which the institution has accepted that other agencies may ignore or may not be equipped to handle such as draft-counseling and providing information on drugs.

Most of the administrator's functions are more action-oriented than those Blocker and his associates describe. Student activism and confrontation occupy a significant portion of his time. Social welfare involvements, illustrated by special state and federal programs (Division of Vocational Rehabilitation, Work Incentive Program, Manpower Development Training Act, New Careers, Veterans, Day Care), also require that he develop special skills which a few years ago were not necessary in the college. The community college president, dean, and other administrators for that matter must be accessible to faculty, students, and representatives of the public at a moment's notice, often at the expense of scheduled activities. Daily, the president is called upon to be an expert in race relations, to be familiar with the various minority cultures in the community he serves, and to understand a whole new vocabulary composed of the slang, colloquialisms, and special vernaculars of blacks, Orientals, Chicanos, and Native Americans (formerly American Indians). And new groups are making demands each day. At Seattle Central Community College, for example, the gypsies, who were previously silent, have made demands just as did minority groups before them, and they should. But what community college administrator knows anything about gypsies? He should if they are a part of the community he is serving.

In his own academic community he is deeply involved in aspects of education which previously were not part of the environment. He has to deal with trade unions, join apprenticeship committees and other such groups with which he has had very little experience. Teacher militancy, negotiations, sanctions, strikes, and the other adversarial roles and positions normally found in labor-management confrontations are other examples. Poorly negotiated contracts between faculty groups and community college districts from New York to Seattle are evidence that community college administrators do not know what they are doing in the negotiation process. This is well documented in the collective bargaining contracts found in Michigan, California, New York, and Illinois (Bolman, 1968, p. 181). They have permitted faculty and others to negotiate and win all kinds of fringe benefits and to establish impregnable safeguards for themselves, while negotiating away many of the rights and safeguards of the students to be taught, others in the academic community, and the citizens who pay the bills. And the agency shop, in my view, has taken away the rights of many teachers. The demand by faculty members to approve administrators takes away the rights of the board of trustees, and banning all derogatory material about a teacher from his personnel files protects incompetent teachers from the scrutiny of the public.

As a result, administrators are called upon to defend decisions made by power-centered faculties—decisions which are often under attack by students, legislators, taxpayers, and other concerned and affected people. In many cases the administrators have been excluded during the formulation of these decisions, even though they are asked to commit their institutions to changes which are not likely to occur and to commit resources which are not available. In fact, "the administrator's position today resembles that of a hospital administrator who keeps the institution running so that the doctors are better able to cure the patients" (Cohen, 1969). In spite of many administrators' accepting this same type of position, some faculties still vote no confidence in them (presidents and deans) (Bolman, 1968, p. 181). They are too often forced to make decisions in the absence of research (Cohen, 1969, p. 102). Community college administrators must walk a tightrope between faculty types: liberal and conservative, hawk and dove, antagonist and pacifist, academic and vocational, competent and incompetent, full time and part time, old and young, dedicated and uncommitted. Each has certain expectations of the administrator to which he is constantly requested to address himself. Can he?

The two-year college administrator, regardless of where he is in the hierarchy, also has to quickly identify and be keenly aware of the students in his institution. On the surface, this should not be difficult. For more than ten years individuals and organizations have been defining the community college student (Medsker, 1960; Knoell, 1966, 1968, 1970; Thornton, 1966; Medsker and Tillery, 1971; Moore, 1970a; Carnegie Commission on Higher Education, 1970; American College Testing Program; American Association of Junior Colleges). Summarily, the administrator soon learns that the community college student is not the "carefully screened, homogeneously prepared, college-oriented student who until a decade or two ago represented the 'typical' college student" (Garrison, 1968, p. 6). While the admissions profile of the community college student is atypical of students in higher education as a whole, the administrator must always be aware of the other characteristics which delineate his variant student population: the apathetic and the complacent, the rebellious, the idealistic, and the confused. He must determine who will tolerate the rigid and prescriptive regulations of the college and who, by the sheer loudness of their voices and the aggressiveness of their behavior, will demand some permissiveness. Although most educators think they are fair and boast of their equalitarian behavior, some students are treated more permissively than are others. Some individuals are permitted to break the rules, while others are not. Neither laws nor rules are consistently applied with impartiality. Administrators, like other people, have sanctioned student misconduct, have relieved students of responsibility for their behavior, and have suspended the rules often.

Students expect the community college administrator to be cool under fire, be able to give and take in a rap session, to hold his own with moderates and extremists, centrists and wingers, coalitionists and purists. They expect him to have a personal stand and to have integrity and guts enough to proclaim it. The administrative position and decisions of a good administrator do not always necessarily correspond to his personal persuasion; and students do not always agree with him, but they do respect him.

The administrator also finds himself submerged in the day-to-day realities of modern life. He must listen to, respond to, and work with the man in the field, the expert from the street. His personal contacts with workers and those of other social classes are as varied as the blue, white, open, and reversed collars they wear.

He deals with architects, building contractors, labor union people, contract service personnel, the clergy, and other special interest groups. Some say to him, "Support your local police," and demand that he fly the flag and command his students and staff to "love it or leave it." Others yell "Right on!"

The proprietors of a "mom and pop" pharmacy, the clerk in a country feed store, the owner of a delicatessen, as well as the president of a food store chain must know him. Old ladies from neighborhood women's clubs drop in and request a part of his time, and he has to be generous with it. The two-year college man or woman also must interact with academic colleagues and a professional community. He cannot be isolated from either the people or the environment he serves. Conversely, the four-year college man or woman deals with professionals who train others to be professionals; he or she works primarily with a professional clientele in a professional community.

Another of the administrator's functions is to anticipate charges of bigotry, and other racial problems in the institution. Campbell and others (1971) point out that race relations is one of two important tensions most basic to school operation. The administrator's own attitude or the bigoted behavior of those on the staff or both will be questioned. Nonwhite students look for symptoms of discrimination. They check to see whether they are represented among the counselors, instructors, secretaries, administrators, and other staff. They attempt to determine how much is being spent on grants and aid for their groups and what recruiting is done of their groups. They watch the teaching and administrative staff—not the students—to see the models these groups set both socially and professionally. They want to know what biases and prejudices are present in the institution with regard to the academically different—the high-risk, disadvantaged, and minority group students. They watch and listen for the slightest infraction and report it to the administration for action. If no action is taken, they often take the matter in their own hands and may solicit assistance from the community. What can the administrator do to minimize the bigotry or the charges of bigotry in his institution?

Blind Man on a Freeway

A long-time administrator in an institution has trouble enough trying to perform these functions. The predicament of a new administrator who comes in from the outside and is met by entrenched faculty, rigid structure, and other powerful administrators above and below him is even greater. The outsider finds himself not knowing whom to fear, whom to placate; who has influence; who hunts, fishes, bowls, golfs, and plays bridge together. He does not know who has a pipeline to somebody who influences his job. In every college the empire builders have small (and sometimes large) niches of the institution under their control; they are the typical obstructionists found throughout education in both administration and faculties. One of the decisions the newcomer has to make is how, when, and if he can make changes in the institution—or, at least, changes in that part of the college within his purview. The disciples of the man who vacated the position often resent him and cannot be expected to be oversolicitous in providing assistance. And those who did not like the predecessor discover how wonderful he was when the new boss rocks the boat too much.

One of the gravest problems new community college administrators (and older ones too) have is establishing and maintaining credibility. They, like other educators, are neither taught in administrative-training programs nor encouraged when they join a college staff to be open with the people who support them. Consequently, they tend not to keep the public informed about what is wrong in their institutions. They do not analyze, criticize, and condemn that which they find amiss in their colleges and make it public record. They do not dare. Some observers call this lack of audit educational malpractice. It is left to concerned legislators, revolting taxpayers, and angry students to call administrators and other educators to account; but these groups do not always get direct answers if, indeed, they get any answers at all. As one Asian student who was demanding more Asian studies courses complained, "Ask one of those guys [an administrator] a question, and he answers with a snow job. First off, he tells you he has to wait until all of the facts are in. But the facts never come in. They just hope you forget to ask about it again. Just a simple question and you get a rain forest of rhetoric." Administrators are criticized for spending too much time postulating, justifying, defending, rationalizing, prophesying, making excuses. People—especially students—are tired of excuses.

Citizens often do not know how to check on the activities of college personnel because educators (both administrators and teachers) do not have monitoring agencies such as physicians and lawyers have in their medical and bar associations—associations with nationally accepted codes of conduct for their membership. Although in rare cases teachers withhold tenure from a coworker, they usually do not have the authority, want the responsibility, or exhibit the desire to expel their fellow professionals from their ranks when the latter are accused of incompetence or wrongdoing. Other groups do take these steps—at least when a member gets caught, thus giving the people who pay the bills an opportunity to see some attempt at professional audit. In education, on the contrary, the response to inquiry is usually defensive, nebulous, or circuitous.

One of the criticisms lay people make of teaching personnel, for example, is that they teach too few hours per week to do an effective job. Many faculty members insist that the number of contact hours they teach is too many to provide effective instruction. Administrators have neither substantiated the faculty claim nor refuted, with evidence, the charges of the critics. Rather than explain, usually both administrators and faculty resort to subterfuge, professional jargon, defensiveness, and other techniques of evasion. These are ill advised tactics. Lay people want straight answers.

Another problem closely connected with that of credibility is the use of the college as a forum for propaganda by students, faculty, and administrators. Students from both inside and outside the institution and from both sides of center make use of college resources and vulnerability to promote their philosophies, air their grievances, protest inequities, and exhibit their frustrations. They use the war in Vietnam, the draft, racism, women's liberation, the deterioration of the cities, injustice, the lack of communication between generations, black studies, the military-industrial complex, the absence of statesmanship among our elected representatives, crime in the streets, drug proliferation, fear, day care needs, and many other reasons for their activities. They pass out leaflets, publish underground newspapers, and infiltrate the legitimate student newspaper and use it for propaganda. Cafeterias, lounges, and many other student gathering places are saturated with speakers who represent all sides of every issue. Walls, fences, sidewalks, chalkboards, windows, and automobiles, even churches, are the surfaces on which scribes leave their messages. No place is sacred.

Although student activism is not as great in the community college as it is in the university (Wilcox, 1968) or as intense as in previous years, the administrator of a two-year college who is involved in confrontation and barraged with propaganda can take little comfort in the documentation, particularly if his institution is in an urban area or is close to a senior college. When senior colleges and universities are nearby, the administrator can expect to find large numbers of students from these institutions on the campus of his college (Lombardi, 1969). Some of them have transferred from the senior college. (In fact, so many students have flunked out, have dropped out, or have been pushed out of the university into the community college that the latter—not the former—is called the real transfer institution by two-year college people.) In spite of the low level of activity, nonstudents from radical organizations are around the campus. The various minority groups can also be found on campus carrying on the same kinds of propaganda activities. All these students are capable of using some minor issues —parking, food in the lunchroom, bookstore prices—to create confrontations with the administration, but other issues are their real concerns.

The revolving student body and the demands that such a mobile group makes are a problem that neither the secondary school principal nor the university president has to face. In a three-year period, the student body of Seattle Central Community College changed the priorities each year. The first year they demanded that the priority item be a new parking lot; the second year, they demanded construction of a student union building; by the third year, the parking lot was again the first priority. During this time, a series of similar demands changed even faster, even though many of these items required long-term commitment.

Just as the students use the community college as a forum for propaganda, so do some members of the faculty use the college and their classrooms for their personal benefit and to support their philosophies. Tunnell (1967) notes these behaviors in faculty and how they influence and, indeed, directly involve students in their issues.

They [faculty] want adequate salaries, retirement, and pension rights, tenure, moderate—indeed small—teaching loads, time for private creative scholarship of their own, sabbaticals, travel allowances, eminent colleagues, handsome, efficient, and convenient buildings and equipment, and apparatus of the most modern and expensive kinds. Many of these items had no place in the simple communities of scholars which they nostalgically recall and quite fancifully dream of reconstituting. Unfortunately, some of these faculty occasionally reveal these discomforts of their souls—sometimes only tacitly—to students. Students are ever sensitive to moods. So what perhaps has only smoldered within the tutor's breast frequently becomes the battle cry of the undergraduate organizer. And the faculty are not always so restrained. They sometimes frankly set out to work up excitement.

Administrators commonly charge that, under the protection of academic freedom, tenure, and no evaluation, some members of the teaching staff openly condemn and criticize the administration too much in the classroom. Kelley and Wilbur (1970, p. 195) have documented faculty criticism of administrators. Administrators also charge that instructors use their teaching time to conduct giant rap sessions and reward or, more accurately, bribe the students into concealing their behavior by awarding good grades. They thus feed the students' egos and neglect their minds. Administrators generally feel they can expect this behavior more from instructors in the college parallel program (especially those in the humanities and social sciences) than from teachers in the vocational or community service programs.

Certain members of the faculty also commonly ask students for support in strikes and other protests over wages, fringe benefits, and working conditions. The following written appeal was issued to the students of one college:

At a collegewide meeting . . . the faculty voted to strike against the college if the Board of Trustees refuses to present us with a reasonable contract proposal for the coming year. We have taken this step only after serious, careful consideration and only because the Board of Trustees has given us no other alternative. Beginning in the first week of April and continuing until late Tuesday night, May 19th, the faculty negotiation team has met with the administration and the Board of Trustees in an attempt to work out a just contract for the faculty. . . . These negotiations, however, have proved fruitless. Unlike the past two years, when collective bargaining was successfully carried on and fair contracts were written, negotiations this year have been marked by the Board's unwillingness to do anything which it feels would offend the "public mood." As a result, the faculty has been presented with a contract proposal that would do away with our agreements of the past two years. While such a contract would offend no one outside the college, it would benefit no one within it. As a matter of simple fact, what we have been asked to accept is a contract that would discredit education at this college for years to come. The Board of Trustees may call this pure imagination, but when the faculty is told that it will be required to structure its classes according to a psychological theory that students are not people but "subjects" who do not think but only have "responses" and when the faculty is told that it will work an "eight-hour shift" and be responsible to "management," then we begin to despair that this Board of Trustees and this administration will ever understand what we, as students and teachers, are really trying to do. So we disagree with the Board on the matter of a philosophy of education. We want to be free to work with our students in the way we think best. We see the Board's proposal as an attempt to make us conform to a so-called systems approach to learning. In plain terms this means that all of us—teachers and students—will be made to conform to one rigid view of education, one standard of values, and one kind of objective. This we absolutely reject. Our strike vote is not based solely on money matters. It is true that we are asking for a raise, but we are more than willing to settle this matter with a cost-of-living increment. So far, however, the Board has flatly rejected anything beyond their proposal of a possible 2 per cent salary increase. The details of our differences with the Board of Trustees are open to your study. In the next few days we will inform you fully of where we stand, what issues are at stake, and how your welfare will be affected by what happens to us. Right now we need your support. Part of our proposal to the Board of Trustees will include a demand that students who support us in the event of a strike be granted complete amnesty when the strike is over. Those teachers who may have to strike are unanimous in their decision that no student will suffer because of our action. If picket lines are formed, we ask you to honor them. To ensure the welfare of both students and teachers, this strike must be complete. And it must be successful. In order to achieve that, we must work cooperatively. We want to say to you, finally, that our stand involved fundamental ideas of education. Neither student nor teachers could survive in the atmosphere which the Board's proposal would create; and if we survived, survival would be all that any of us would have. In taking the stand which we have chosen, this faculty is in your debt. Your recent peaceful protests and those of students like you nationwide, which were the products of a strong commitment to principles, have encouraged us to stand on our principles. In this you have been our teachers, and you have taught us well.

This open letter came from a few faculty members without the knowledge of the entire faculty and was not signed. Much of the content of the letter was untrue. It was accompanied with petitions

17

for students to sign. A number of students complained to administrators about this activity on the part of their teachers.

I'm in Psychology 105. I want to know why you allow that teacher in there to constantly take the class time to solicit student help so he can fatten his pocketbook. He actually had the nerve to ask us to sign a petition.

You don't need him [the instructor] around. He spends all of his time bad-mouthing you and the college. He lectured the whole class period, again, about the administration being unfair. And, then, he had the gall to ask us to sign a petition to support them if they strike.

I hate being used, man; that's what I hate. I hate being used. That honkie got us in the class and tried to talk us to death about the administration and the board. Soon as he got through running it down to us, he springs this petition on us and suggested—you get that, man, suggested—that we might want to support them—voluntarily, of course. That stud was 'bout as subtle as a fart in a crowded room. Everybody knew where he was coming from. All he was interested in was in sweetenin' his hip [getting money].

Other students freely signed the documents; and still others felt that they were pressured by their instructors to sign the petitions:

If the teachers stay out a long time, I can't get out of my program on schedule. So I signed it.

I signed it because I don't want to make the instructor mad. I need the grade. It probably won't make any difference anyway.

I don't like being blackmailed into doing anything. When I get out of this course, I'm going to tell that S.O.B. a thing or two.

When it comes to involving students in faculty-administration conflict, no teacher is as deadly and as effective in creating confusion and confrontation as a psychology teacher with a problem.

Administrators as Blind Men

Faculty members also solicit the aid of students to push, pressure, and negotiate for the administrative pattern typical of the four-year college or university. They want power placed in the hands of the faculty rather than in the administration. As Charles Hurst, president of Malcolm X Community College in Chicago and a member of the board of directors of the American Association of Junior Colleges (AAJC), put it to the members of the Student Personnel Commission at the 1971 annual AAJC Convention in Washington, D.C., "the administrators are then tigers without teeth or claws." Some faculty also use students to help apply pressure to force school closures during crises such as during the Kent State and Jackson State tragedies in the spring of 1970 or during a heavy snowfall. In short, the community college administrator soon learns that some of his teaching colleagues are not as professional as one might expect.

Administrators also use the college and its resources to propagandize. They tend not to be as direct in their activities as students and faculty are. Yet they are quite effective. Sometimes they work through staff meetings. Some know how to use a newsletter effectively. Others have discovered that a well designed business form can not only sell an idea but also control a situation. A clever administrator can work through the student newspaper. If he is smart, he goes through the "Letters to the Editor" instead of the headlines and editorials.

Administrators are bureaucrats. Call them by their titles: dean, division chairman, registrar, controller, administrative assistant, and so forth. They control the nuts and bolts of the day-to-day operations, and bureaucrats resist change. As such, some of them may not be concerned with the over-all goals of their colleges. "They want to preserve their little empires and run their operations with a minimum of disruption. Any change—regardless of how good it may be for the organization or the people it should serve—is perceived as a threat, and they will undercut policies, conceal information, and mislead their superiors to protect themselves and their positions" (Schoonmaker, 1971, p. 4).

The way an administrator supports or fails to support the

19

authority above him is one of the ways he can push one posture while blocking others. For example, in an unpopular directive or policy, a president or a dean can point out to those administrators below him (or to faculty) who challenge or question the directive that those above him are responsible for its content and demands. He can suggest that grievances come to him in writing with copies going to those who supervise him.

An administrator can develop and maintain control in still other ways. He can praise programs and people if he likes them; and he can condemn or criticize or simply ignore projects and individuals he does not like. Not infrequently, one administrator convinces other members of the administrative staff of his position before he goes into a meeting so that the group is unified before the alternatives or the proposals are submitted. Some gain control by taking advantage of a new superior's lack of knowledge and committing him to projects he has not had enough time to understand. The following excerpt from a memorandum written by an associate dean to a new president illustrates this latter point: "I recommend that we assign the responsibilities of *acting chairman* of dental technology to Esther Wagstaff. This responsibility was performed last year by Phillip Wilkins, the assistant dean. I recommend that Mrs. Wagstaff's salary be prorated on 222 days from where she is now located on the salary schedule, plus the increases that the other chairmen receive." The dean was trying to do many things with this memorandum. By suggesting that the position be an acting one without indicating a time limitation, he ensured that he could always use the threat of removal with the person involved and have her support when he needed it. His suggestion of additional salary further obligated her. He was thus solidifying his own position by placing a person he could control in a sensitive position. This associate dean had created all five similar positions on the college staff, and some of these acting positions had been held for as long as three years. Since he was a liaison person, he thereby controlled the communication flow in two directions.

Administrators use propaganda in other ways too. Some deans and division/department chairmen who work directly with

20

advisory committees generate support for their own ideas through these committees. Some of them are willing to overlook incompetence in staff members while making those people commit themselves to continued support of certain ideas, policies, and practices. Other administrators leak pertinent information, which can cause many problems in the institution. Some administrators praise the college during the time they are actively in the college community then methodically malign it when they are asked about it by their neighbors. (This behavior on the part of administrators was alluded to many times during the Minority Affairs Conference at Seabeck Resort near Bremerton, Washington, in September 1970.) This two-faced behavior happens most with people who work in an urban college and live in the suburbs. Know anybody like this?

If the foregoing descriptions of functions and problems are accurate at all, it should be understandable why the community college administrator spends so little time at what many consider his primary job—improving the quality of education or, more precisely, improving instruction. The improvement of instruction includes not only what the administrator is able to do with the academic professionals but also what he can do with the learning environment to make it useful to both the teacher and the student.

Traditionally, an administrator's primary job was providing good supervision of instruction—that is, making available the resources necessary to improve the educational climate and providing opportunities for individual and professional growth in the staff that he supervised. He and his assistants visited classrooms frequently to observe the teaching and learning process; he checked failure lists, absentee lists, and dropout rates. He had on file a copy of each instructor's syllabi. Each year he evaluated the faculty with the knowledge of the individual teachers. If he was concerned about an individual's performance, together they evolved ways to change that performance. In some colleges the administrator was also a teacher. In fact, the early colleges did not have administrators (Horn, 1962, p. 55).

Just as community college administrators today know that while in college they were not trained to be administrators in the institution they serve, they are equally aware that two-year college teachers were not taught to teach community college students—that is, they were not taught to diagnose learning problems or to deal with special learning problems. They were not taught to construct tests and evaluate students, to deal with individual differences, to motivate young adults, to use a variety of teaching strategies, or to provide a good reward system (other than grades). Since the administrator has not been taught to perform these tasks either unless he did graduate work in elementary education, he is hardly in a position to give knowledgeable evaluations or to offer suggestions. Both the administrator and the teacher would do well to take a few lessons from their counterparts in the elementary schools.

Other reasons the administrator does so little to improve instruction are that he is always an outsider to the faculty and that his college is controlled to a great extent by outside forces. The administrator has (or takes) little time to visit classrooms and teachers, and when he does, he gets permission. He is usually not invited by faculty to get involved in the development of curricula, to meet with division and department faculties, to take part in research in the institution within his area of academic expertise, to help in the selection of new equipment and educational hardware, to exchange ideas, or to join the faculty senate. (This statement obviously does not apply to division and department chairmen, who are—or should be—intimately involved in planning. Many of them teach.) Little, if anything, is asked of the administrator beyond noninterference and complete support. It is an accepted axiom that the administrator's job is to get the money and get out of the way. One dean notes: "I might beat the drums and the bush to get interest, cash, space or whatever else is needed to get reform underway." Others say that "they often work on the academic deans to induce them to provide . . . the money to implement new ideas" (Heiss, 1970).

In some colleges, it is not only a matter of principle but also a tradition never to ask the administrator for advice on instruction. At one college, the president is a nationally known media expert and has written two books on the subject. Since he knew there was a problem in the college media center, he offered his services to the staff and the faculty. He got no response. Several weeks later, he was introduced to a consultant who came to assist the campus with its media. The president was delighted to see his former student, but he was disturbed (and he should have been) that the resources of the college were being spent for expert advice that was already available on campus. Fortunately, he had the sense and courage to be angry and the security to be arbitrary. He issued a directive indicating that college funds would not be spent for expertise already available from the administration or the faculty, although he did realize that special situations could arise and stated that provisions would be made for them. In Washington, this activity was so rampant in the state colleges that Mike Layton, a reporter for the *Daily Olympian,* wrote a series of articles on the practice. Following his expose an organized group of concerned citizens brought enough pressure on the state legislators and through them the college administrations to force them to stop the featherbedding that was taking place among college staffs.

With regard to outside forces and the role they play in the instructional process, it is well established that many extrainstitutional forces determine the curriculum. Universities; technical, vocational, and industrial agencies; traditions; legislators; booster clubs; economic and social situations all influence the curriculum of the college—and should. Administrators should be aware of the effects these demands have on institutions since some of these outside forces have more to say about what goes on in specific areas of instruction than administrators do. The apprenticeship program is a case in point.

Other problems plague community college administrators, among them the economic recession which has hit higher education. Inflation, greed, poor and archaic management, coupled with increased enrollment and building on soft money (government and foundation funds), have created financial problems for administrators the likes of which we have never experienced before. The sixties —the period of greatest growth—provided higher education, including the community colleges, with a privileged and patrician existence. Administrators as much as any other group profited and encouraged the windfalls and equally abused them. They did not exercise financial caution.

This lack of caution manifested itself in other ways. In the sixties community college administrators, particularly in large public school systems, supported teacher militancy. They were among the educational Machiavellians who helped to give the financial scent to school personnel by encouraging teachers to demand higher salaries and greater fringe benefits. The administrators knew that they, too, would profit from the financial fallout, and they did. When faculty members got more money, so did they. The supervisors did not know, however, that once the teachers made a kill they would not be satisfied. The smell of blood lingered. And the administrator who, for his own gain, once nurtured the predators now finds himself among the prey.

A final problem I would like to discuss in this chapter is relations with boards of trustees because the actions of trustees (either as individual members or as a body) can make the life of an administrator—especially the president—one of continuous success or of perpetual adversity. The members of a board are like those who represent the public elsewhere. Some of them are well informed, make well thought-out decisions, define their roles, understand their responsibilities, give their support freely, impose certain standards of behavior upon themselves, demand a definite quality of performance from their administrative officers, are ever aware of the public trust and the rights of various groups (students, faculty, administration), and are keenly conscious of institutional resources and how they are handled. Others are a pain in the administration. There is little point in discussing here what good boards do. Shakespeare has already advised us of what happens to the good that men do. The obligation of this volume is to identify those structures which cause the administrator stress and make the job of supervision and service difficult if not impossible. The board of trustees can be—and often is—one such structure.

The amount of administrative time it takes to work out the problems created by a meddling board (or an individual board member) is exorbitant. The effect on administrative and staff morale is incalculable. Administrators are afraid to make decisions; policies and procedures are worthless; faculty, students, and others become insubordinate; and the entire staff is subject to unexpected work loads, attacks from various groups, lawsuits, and so forth. No college president who is worth his salt and who therefore can find another job remains in such a situation.

In all fairness to boards of trustees, it must be said that some take over the leadership in a college because the administrative officers do not. Other boards are political appointees or are elected to represent special interest groups. In certain states, politics play such an important role that board members can recruit and hire faculty members, can fire individuals because of personal dislikes, and so on, until the institution reeks with nepotism and other such preferential selection and retention of staff. Under these conditions, one can understand some of the behavior of these groups even though these activities are to be condemned not condoned.

Community college boards of trustees function differently from four-year boards. They come from the local community. They meet monthly. They may know many members of the administrative staff and faculty, and thus their decisions may be more social than educational. They are lay people who rarely know what is going on in an institution and depend upon the administration to guide them and keep them informed. (If the administrator fails to do this, he gets what he deserves when something goes wrong or when his services are terminated.) Although board members do not like to think of themselves as rubber stamps, they often are. They usually have neither the background nor the opportunity to become as informed as they need to be to make quality educational decisions. But they can learn.

In view of all of the problems discussed here, it is readily observable that the community college administrator has a unique role and function. His role is different from the long evolved, well organized, and well developed principalship; and it is different from the highly academic and departmentalized deanship. It is appropriate to explore the reasons why the tasks of these two administrators are so different from those of the community college administrator.

American education has evolved with only one school administrator theoretically and practically trained to do his job—the principal. (Many would say that the superintendency is equally as well defined, but the principal and the superintendent normally receive identical training.) The public elementary or high school principal is better prepared to do his job than are administrators in the other areas of education. Prior to his elevation to the principalship he is a classroom teacher. In the better school systems he is also required to be a reading clinician. He is eventually promoted to administrative assistant and learns to take care of the book inventory, average the daily attendance, and perform other record-keeping chores. The young administrative assistant learns also to mark teachers according to the criteria for recommending tenure and to construct a well organized but flexible educational program; he knows from his previous teaching experience how to manage a classroom, to adjust instruction to the abilities of the pupils; and if he is in the elementary school, he can substitute when a regular teacher is out. He knows and frequently uses the achievement, cumulative, and anecdotal records of pupils in school. He is well acquainted with the instructional aids used in his school (textbooks, supplementary books, guidebooks and manuals, audiovisual aids, radio and television programs). He is familiar with grading and promotion policies, with all the board of education rules, as well as with state rules and regulations; and he performs many other miscellaneous jobs. The principal knows the community where he works, the general characteristics of the people, and other information which assists him in performing his job.

The requirements are rigid. In order to qualify, particularly in many large urban school systems, the prospective principal must pass an examination. In St. Louis, for example, a candidate for the principalship is required to pass the National Teachers Examination with a score of 550 (fifty points higher than that required for a teacher) to qualify to take the administration section of the examination. He is also required to have a specified number of guidance, supervision, and administration credits to obtain state certification. The student (or teacher) training to be a principal learns about test construction, techniques and methods of teaching, child and adolescent psychology, mental hygiene, learning theory, and so forth. Principals are also required to have administrators' credentials, but the same requirements are not mandatory for four-year college administrators. With all the principal has to do, he has to be a good administrator. In some large city schools his enrollment is as large as that in many small colleges. Sometimes he has an administrative assistant or vice-principal, although in smaller communities he often does not have assistance. He and his staff must then become registrar, admissions officer, placement person, testing division, and so forth. The principal, at least, has learned to do the job.

On the contrary, the chief administrator in a four-year college or university may not have any background and experience in running an educational institution at all. We have generals, ministers, businessmen, hustlers, and others heading colleges and universities. College presidents are normally isolated and insulated from the faculty, students, and others in the academic community. They deal with corporation presidents, high government officials, big industrialists, alumni organizations, boards of regents, and other people far removed from the plebeian running of the institution. They are probably more aware of the financial aspects of the institution than of any other facet. Rarely does one know anything about the program of his institution. He does not get involved in guiding and directing what is happening. Moreover, in some of the larger institutions, he has a whole group of vice-presidents and public relations people to keep him looking good and to keep the public happy. As Parkinson (1970) states:

The theoretical responsibilities of the modern college president may rank second in importance to the governor, his domain often including a city as well as a campus. He will hold sway over faculty and student bodies numbering in the thousands, over nuclear accelerators and playing fields, a football stadium and a concert hall, a radio station and an experimental farm. He may have his

27

own police force and fire brigade, his own newspaper and airfield, his own shopping center and club. He does everything but mint a coinage in his own effigy. Yet, in sharp contrast with an admiral or a general, he has never been specifically trained, assessed, or scientifically chosen.

The deans and other administrators in colleges and universities are, for the most part, academicians. There is an assumption that academic accomplishments qualify academicians to serve as administrators. Good administrators selected from these candidates are exceptions (Ingraham and King, 1968, p. 196). Some of them may have studied the theory of administration, but a significant number have not worked as administrators outside the colleges and universities where they are currently assigned (Heiss, 1970; Enarson, 1962). Deans, traditionally, head specific academic departments which have been organized into schools and colleges. They are responsible for the academic program and for coordinating the departments. The problem is that they may not have anything to say about these programs because they have been organized and are controlled by the faculty. In fact, faculties in senior institutions have been given autonomous authority not only over much of the design and administration of curriculum but also over much administrative procedure. Enarson (1962, p. 122) describes the dean's dilemmas of preparation in this way:

The academic dean is not "trained" in any sense for the job. He may have served an apprenticeship as assistant to the president; more commonly he will have been a successful departmental chairman or dean of a college. In any event he is picked because it is felt, always on the basis of too little evidence, that he has administrative ability. . . . We can be certain about one thing: the gap between what he has done and what he is now expected to do is a big one. He may have been a chairman of physics or the dean of the school of education. No matter, he will be woefully unprepared whatever his background. . . . The dean is a man in the middle. In his brief moments of glory, he sees himself as the strong bridge

28

between faculty and president. In grimmer moments, he will feel that a bridge is to walk upon and for some to wipe their muddy feet upon. The dean is forever beset with pressures and problems. He will never have enough money or time or information or patience. If he has vision, his reach will forever exceed his grasp. A Gresham's law of administration will wear upon him; the trivia and the detail will bulk so large that there is never enough time to tackle the larger issues of education. Worst of all, he has substituted the "in and out basket" of the administrator for the quiet of the library, the stimulation of students, the chance to grow in strength and reputation in the field of his choice. Finally, he will find it difficult to be honest with himself and with his colleagues on the very point on which his life now pivots.

From the preceding discussion, we can see how the job of community college administrator differs from the jobs of his two counterparts. Community colleges however usually combine public school and four-year syndromes, and this combination of role finds an echo in the role of the administrator. The public school syndrome is manifest in the open-door policy; the fact that a considerable portion of the teaching staff is often transplanted from public secondary schools; the fact that the college is sometimes under the control of a superintendent; the fact that the students may vary in their abilities from the illiterate to the honor student; and so forth. But most significant, the community college administrators are often thought of as little more than public school principals. Perhaps this idea is to be expected since a few administrators in higher education were originally trained to be principals—not presidents; academicians—not managers; supervisors—not politicians; and thinkers—not fighters. Principals, however, have always had options that community college administrators do not enjoy. They can use the influence of the home and parents to help control the school environment. They can threaten without fear of reprisal and can often apply punishment instead of reason. Principals also have tradition and laws (regardless of their antiquity) to support them; they are often rulers who reign without checks and balances; and they have always had a central administration to stop the buck when they pass it.

To turn now to how the four-year college syndrome manifests itself in community colleges, it is rather common for persons from the senior institutions to migrate into the teaching and administrative ranks of the open-door college. Unfortunately, because of the mystique from above, community college people seem glad to have them. These migrants come unprepared to deal with the kind of students they find. Their research orientation and lack of teaching or administrative training makes them academic snobs or administrative incompetents. The skills that they used in the institution they left are inappropriate for the institution to which they migrate. The liberal arts faculty like, respect, and emulate them; the vocational faculty are suspicious of and frequently reject them; and the community service faculty take them as they are and try to help them become what they can be. This description does not fit every administrator or teacher who has come from a four-year institution, but it does describe many of them.

This four-year syndrome is manifest most in the liberal arts, or college transfer, faculty. I have discussed the symptoms at some length in earlier writings (Moore, 1970a):

There are . . . staff members [community college faculty] whose desires project the university syndrome. They know that the university rewards the researcher, not the teacher; promotes the Ph.D.s, not the teachers (teaching assistants and other holders of the B.A. or M.A. degree) who really carry on the instruction in the institution; they are aware that the awarding of tenure and other fringe benefits goes to the people who give the least amount of time and attention to freshman and sophomore students, not to the teacher who teaches them; and it is well known that the university system honors faculty members who write books and present scholarly (if not relevant) papers—not the teacher who advises and gives his time to his undergraduate students. Faculty members in an increasing number of community colleges attempt to mimic the practices of university faculty. They want the same privileges as

*the four-year faculty without the responsibility of writing, research,
and advance study.*

These faculty members are concerned about rank, teaching assistants, faculty control, subject matter, degrees, selection criteria, test
scores, university demands, tenure, sabbatical leaves, being called
colleagues rather than teachers or coworkers, and many other matters important in the university. The great fear among many administrators in the community college is that the university syndrome
is so entrenched that it may be difficult to reverse.

The community college, then, becomes a hybrid of the university and the common school. It assumes and performs some of
the functions of both these institutions. And thus the administrator
is forced to become principal and president; academician and
manager; supervisor and politician; thinker and fighter without
the defined role and legal backing of the principal or the prestige,
insulation, and almost automatic acceptance of the university president.

Some other questions only the graduate institutions can
answer. One question is: Are graduate schools willing to change
their programs for producing administrators? Another is: Is the
graduate institution going to do any serious research to find out
what kinds of specific skills are needed in the preparation of two-
year school administrators? Will graduate faculties even admit that
better preparation is needed for administrators if they are expected
to move into administrative jobs and do them successfully? The
answers at this juncture are negative. One interested in researching
the answers for himself has but to read the requirements for obtain-
ing a master's or a doctorate in administration today. Then read
what the requirements were ten years ago. He should talk to members of graduate faculties when and if he can find them. He should
take a look at the requirements being evolved for the new, proposed
Doctor of Arts degree. Finally, he should visit a community college
to see what kinds of skills and experiences are necessary to meet
the needs of a community college environment and then compare
them with the kinds of skills and experiences prescribed for an

advanced degree in higher education administration. The administrator in the community college today must be more able to act than to contemplate; more crisis-oriented than long-term–oriented; more able to focus sharply than to see issues in a diffused way. The community college administrator has a more comprehensive job than do the administrators at the other levels of education, and virtually nothing has been done to train him. Whether one looks ahead or looks back, there is little movement in the direction of appropriate training for the job. At best, he has only a white cane.

Finally, the community college administrator must accept the reality that he is usually either the villain or the scapegoat. He can be both. Depending upon where he is in the hierarchy, he must be prepared to deal with angry students, assorted demands, racism, tradition, budget cuts, unions, faculty senate, board of trustees, the public, the press, the legislature, and other administrators. In spite of these sometimes adversarial components, he must keep uppermost in his mind that the improvement of the quality of education is his main objective. This is difficult. When one is up to his ass in alligators, it is easy to forget that his original objective was to drain the swamp.

New Students, New Faculty, New Demands

TWO

Of all the situations the community college administrator has to face, one of the most pervasive is his dealings with the new constituencies on campus—student activists, women's liberation, minority groups, and militant faculty. In his relations with all these groups, the administrator constantly has to cope with a series of management and human relations problems and has to make decisions affecting others who, in turn, affect him.

Student involvement, for example, now requires special administrative skills which were not needed a decade ago. Students are speaking out on issues that concern them and their education, and the administrator had better listen. They are often heard at meetings of the community college board of trustees and in the offices of the president, the dean, and other decision makers. Students participate in the formulation of policies; their delegations sit down with governors and legislators to press for laws favorable to

33

themselves and to the community college. They are making a contribution to community college life; their inputs are sought if not always welcomed. The administrator who deals with them must be able to change often in response to their changes, and to respond accurately he must have constant feedback. If administrators were getting feedback and the right kind, perhaps they would not be in the turmoil in which they presently find themselves. If they were aware of what students were thinking, they might be able to meet some of the students' needs. The administrator responds to the faculty when they express themselves. When the community speaks out, he responds to their inquiries and charges. Only when students speak out has he found that he does not know how to respond because there is no adequate feedback system between students and the administration. If an administrator was taught how to develop and use a good feedback system, he could act rather than react, stimulate rather than respond, anticipate rather than be shocked, deal with minor problems before they became crisis situations.

The need for such a feedback system is especially crucial when dealing with the new constituencies mentioned above, and the administrator has to develop many other skills for relating to these groups. Let us look first at student activists and the problems they pose for the community college administrator.

A board of trustees or a president or a dean gives an administrator his job. Make no mistake about it, the students, faculty, and community allow him to keep it. In order to make the job easier than it may otherwise be there are some things that he can do. In an urban community college, the administrator should make one of his first orders of business getting to know the militant and dissident organizations (on the left and the right) inside and outside the institution. They will do more than most to prevent him from performing the job he was hired to do. Although the overt and disruptive behavior of these students has decreased since the spring of 1970, their activities are by no means ended. Their tactics are just different. Now they intimidate and threaten with various kinds of extortion and blackmail. It is incalculable value for the administrator to meet the leaders of the various organizations and to know their addresses, phone numbers, and philosophies since he may find it necessary to contact them many times. Therefore, one of his priorities should be to arrange appointments and then to visit the headquarters of the various organizations in order to sit down and engage in dialogue. These visits should be made as soon as the administrator comes on the job, even before he accepts the position. Prior to the meeting he should attempt to find out about the group. There are many sources for this information. He can start with old copies of the school newspaper, underground publications, and the daily newspaper. If the organization produces a special publication, he can read it and all other material he can get on the organization. Meeting announcements on the bulletin board provide him with information and he can accept and read some of the literature passed out constantly in and around his institution. He can talk with members of the staff who may know some of the students. He can check dissident or activist files, which every school has or should have. Other students may provide him with information. He can check with the police department; and he can check with one of the best sources—the secretaries.

He should carry with him all the material he has at his disposal which describes and defines the parameters of his job. He should make available to the group copies of all of the state, local, and college laws, codes, statutes, rules, and regulations; bargaining agreements; specifications if new buildings are planned; and other pertinent information. If the groups know what is in the realm of possibility for the administrator, they save him and themselves many future anxieties because they are aware of the demands he cannot meet. They instead look for the source of power—the board of trustees or regents or some state agency. In these meetings the administrator cannot commit the institution to anything except that which is defined in the college guidelines and in the description of his job. This point should be made quite clear. Since he has presented the group with copies of his job description and copies of statutes and other documents which define the limits of his authority and power, he does not have to spend excessive time attempting to outline his official function.

Blind Man on a Freeway

When an administrator meets with one of the groups, preferably on their ground, he can employ a variety of tactics. He should listen most of the time. Although aware that many young people need and want direction, he should never attempt to give the members the well known snow job. He is talking with people who have mastered the technique of mesmerizing—both as perpetrators and detectors. He should also avoid conveying the idea that he is there to help the listeners. He is there to help himself; he needs them more than they need him. Yet, he should not get defensive when they charge that both the institution and the society are racist and sick. There is little value in getting into this type of argument. Even if the charges are true, he did not single-handedly make either the institution or the society the way it is. He cannot be the scapegoat for an entire society. Nor can he change it single-handedly. The administrator must stand his ground and be his own man. He cannot whine, beg, or apologize. He should be aware that for every question students ask or threat they make there is a legitimate question he can ask or appeal he can make in return. For example, if they threaten to burn down the institution, he can appeal to their sense of humanity, suggest the irrationality of the act, indicate the consequences of the crime; or he can be firm and say what one black administrator said to a group of black militants who attempted to intimidate him with such a threat: "Burn the motherfucker down. I don't own it!" (There is nothing like an understanding among men.) The sheer shock of hearing this educator, this academician, this college leader evoke such epithets was enough to turn the interrogation around. The militants knew immediately that the administrator was well aware of who they were and how they operated. With that one well chosen statement, this administrator had won. In spite of this particular administrator's success in dealing with this specific group of black militants, most black administrators know and most white ones must be constantly reminded that a black face is not a passport in the black community. It must also be clearly understood here that although "minority students have indeed been responsible for some campus disruptions, . . . more intensive coverage of student unrest has revealed that black students, by and large,

36

are concerned with acquiring an education; the typical disrupter is white and middle class" (Newman, 1971).

Whereas the administrator may have unfair charges leveled against him and may, therefore, be used as the whipping boy for society in this meeting, many of the other charges leveled against him are legitimate. I have participated in these meetings both as a dean and as a college president. As a participant, I have been threatened, ridiculed, cursed, and damned. Yet, in spite of all of their hostility, I know from my own knowledge and experience that the students are more accurate with some of their charges than we like to admit. When they charge that many administrators do not know what is going on in their institutions; that too many of them are rarely visible and accessible; that a large number of them are either unwilling or unable to exert leadership; that they are running scared all the time; that they are like senators, congressmen, and other legislators in that they place their own positions, personal prestige, and the special interest of certain groups above the interest of the students and the other public they are hired to support, serve, and protect; that they take credit for the successes in their institutions but refuse to accept the blame for failures; and that they permit the whole college staff (secretaries, faculty, lunchroom workers, security guards, parking lot attendants, the registrar, and so forth) to brutalize the students—they are right in far too many cases.

It is quite evident in these meetings that both the student radicals and nonstudents are disenchanted with administrators because the latter see things wrong in the institution and do not correct them if they are at all controversial. They point out that administrators go out and hire outside consultants to point out problems and raise issues which should be pointed out and illuminated by the persons responsible for the management of the institution. The administrator pays the expert to tell him what he already knows but still does nothing about the problem.

The administrator must also be genuinely interested in what the group says about itself. He should attempt to determine and understand the goals of the organization; the programs it has; how institution rules and regulations create barriers which prevent the

37

organization from accomplishing its goals; what the communication problems with the institution are; and what kinds of liaison can be set up between the administrator and the group.

Activist groups can (and do) use many tactics to harass the administrator (including recording the meeting on tape), and the administrator can expect to be psychologically leaned on (intimidated) as the individual members interrogate him. But it is very unlikely that he will be intimidated physically. Dissident groups are quick to test the administrator's tolerance level for obscenities, however. Words and phrases which some define as profanity flow from the lips of these young people as easily as nursery rhymes—easier. If the administrator is black, members from black militant groups may call him Uncle Tom, Tom, handkerchief head, oreo, Sambo, and so forth to disconcert him. A white group may call a black administrator a black conservative to his face. Most of them do not openly venture stronger words. It is a mistake for an administrator to try to beat young activists at their game unless his background is such that he can appear comfortable in this activity. Black administrators tend to be better at this game than whites since a significant number of blacks have come from "deprived" communities and ghettos, where a few profanities are not even a mild distraction. Most of them (by no means all) have heard and have used the four-letter words since kindergarten. Blacks also seem to have an unusual ability to understand their own as well as other vernaculars. And there is also an immediate identification among blacks at all levels, perhaps because no black, regardless of his academic and financial stature, is ever more than fifteen minutes ahead of the black without these advantages.

Other tactics are used to try to wear down the administrator. But he should be the last person to suggest that the meeting be terminated, even though he may be the first to want it terminated. He should be prepared to spend as much as four or five hours at the meeting. Activists may take turns questioning him. He may find that he travels the same ground many times. He should get a good night's sleep or take a nap before he reports in order not to be worn down by his hosts.

New Students, New Faculty, New Demands

Activists can test administrators in other ways. The guest can expect to have marijuana smoke blown in his face, and he may be asked to share pot. Even if he smokes pot, he cannot afford to enjoy his host's hospitality. He should turn it down firmly without any word of judgment. On the other hand, if the hosts offer the guest a beer or some other refreshment, he should not hesitate to accept. This can be the first of many times he sits down and shares with the students some refreshment and dialogue; it must happen many times more if he is to be effective. Perhaps more than anything else at these meetings, the administrator is tested by having to listen to all the values and symbols of America—the police, big business, the church, the school system, and so forth—damned by well read, idealistic young people who have been disillusioned by the system. He hears charges that racism, discrimination, poverty, elitism, pollution are perpetrated by a few powerful men and organizations. Books and other resources in the meeting place document these charges.

Finally, trappings of the activists are all about, and some of them are designed to intimidate the administrator. In some group headquarters, firearms are displayed—more for effect than anything else. Lombardi (1969) does an adequate job of describing these trappings:

Characteristic of campus activists is the adoption of insignia of various kinds. Black activists affect African dress, hair styles, beards, earrings, and necklaces with certain charms or emblems attached. Some wear berets, jackets with insignias, and shirts or sweaters with "Black Power," "Malcolm X," or his picture imprinted on them. Many change their names to African. . . . Mexican American and other activists may adopt Castro or Guevara-style beards imitating the "barbudos." Armbands also appear, especially during demonstrations. Few campuses have matched Columbia's five differently colored armbands. Black and brown armbands predominate on junior college campuses. Black, of course, may represent either black students or "mourning" over some alleged objectionable administrative action or decision. Black lapel bars are

39

worn "in mourning" for those killed or maimed in Vietnam. Brown armbands, berets, and jackets similar to those worn by Cuban revolutionists are often worn by Mexican American students. Armbands may be used as insignias for leaders and/or as symbols of membership in or sympathy for the cause. Other equipment of activists includes tables, chairs, signs, and placards, with and without wooden standards, handbills, leaflets, newspapers, bullhorns, and, occasionally, transistor-equipped public address systems. The more extreme groups may display Red, Mexican, or Cuban flags, may carry knives, firearms, or just bullets, or may use bombs and other incendiary materials.

Even forewarned with all of these descriptions, however, the administrator can never fully anticipate what will happen, although he can expect that the group will be surprised; administrators do not usually go to the students and others who have, or will, openly confront them. In general, they play by ear.

One final word of caution is in order. The administrator should always be honest and direct. When one young blond administrator said to a group of activists, "I'm scared, but I'm here," the response from most of the members of the group was "Right on." Activists appreciate such honesty; liars and hypocrites are in for difficulty with these students, particularly with minority students. They have a remarkable ability to cut across verbal charades and other academic distractions, to go directly to a problem, and to define it as they see it in the easiest way. When such groups make requests of an administrator, he should not hesitate to fulfill them if he can. If he cannot, he must not hesitate to say so. When the administrator leaves the meeting, he should take with him all the written material and propaganda available. He should plan to meet with the leaders of the group as often as possible. If the group sponsors a public affair, he should drop in for awhile. His presence is appreciated, and he is well protected. John V. Lindsay of New York exemplifies this kind of community diplomacy. Mayor of the most crime-ridden city in America, he walks the ghetto streets alone and at night. Yet, he does not compromise either his principles or his position to those living in the area. The administrator can establish the same kind of rapport with activist students and non-students. This does not mean that each time he sees activists either he or they will be happy about the encounter. At least each will know the other.

The students and nonstudents who are conservative can be dealt with by the administrator in similar ways, although they present a different problem in some respects. They are not as open, direct, or loud as the leftist students, but in many ways they are more frightening. While the activist students on the left attack inanimate objects (buildings, offices), activist students and nonstudents on the right attack people. These conservative students are different from other activists in other ways. The overwhelming majority of them are white and are the sons and daughters of hard hats, other blue-collar workers, and some white-collar workers. Although enrolled in all programs in the college, they constitute the overwhelming majority of the enrollment in apprenticeship and other vocational programs. They spend their spare time in little huddles in the cafeteria and elsewhere, in contrast to leftist students who are noisy and who are always out drumming up business. Whereas militant leftist students freely include women in their groups, these blue-collar vocational students exclude women students. In addition they do not like students who wear their hair long, mix date, enjoy rock music, or espouse liberal causes.

To identify these students, the administrator needs only to listen to what they say during coffee breaks and at other such times. And there are other ways. Displayed on the automobiles of these students are bumper stickers with rightist slogans such as "support your local police," "love it or leave it," "I fight the war on poverty—I work"; small American flags; gun club decals; and slogans rejecting school busing. These students do not have the political savvy of the militant students. In their political beliefs they represent the fundamentalist point of view. They claim to be law-abiding citizens, and in many ways they are; the administration can count on their support as long as it does not yield in any way to the demands of radical students. Members of the rightist group claim to be 100 per

41

cent American; they recite the Pledge of Allegiance, constantly refer to the Constitution and its guarantee of their rights, support law enforcement, condemn crime in the streets, and champion George Wallace, Spiro Agnew, and, to a lesser degree, Richard Nixon. But in spite of their claim to be 100 per cent American, they are anti-black, antihippie, and anti-Jew; they tend to operate with closed minds. Their solution to the awesome problems of school and society is to incarcerate the people who dissent, to prevent them from gaining employment, to censor the press, and to exterminate dissenters. In short, they are the first to evoke the Constitution and its protection of their rights, while systematically setting about to deprive others of those same rights.

In some parts of the country, the administrator is not likely to be invited into the inner circle of these students and nonstudents, which includes the exterminators, dynamiters, and other such individuals who "support their local police." (There are, to be sure, violent students on the left and the right. The administrator may come to know both.)

If the administrator does meet with the right-wing group, he should be as direct and honest with them as he was with the other groups. He should carry there too laws, codes, statutes, his job description, and all other material which helps him explain the parameters of his job. In like manner, he must make it perfectly clear that he does not intend to show favor to any group. When the administrator visits the militant groups, he is asked what his position is; the rightist groups accept his presence as representing his support for the group. They see him as their inside man. On no condition should he reveal any of the confidences which he has received from one group to the other group. If he has knowledge of extreme violence, he should make this information available only to his supervisor and the proper authorities.

Conservative groups can threaten the administrator the same ways radical groups can. If the administrator is white and refuses to handle blacks in the school the way the right-wing group thinks they should be handled, they may call him a nigger lover and all the other well known and freely used words and phrases that some

42

whites use to describe whites who befriend blacks. If the administrator's response is not to their liking when they ask how he is going to handle students they consider radical, they may threaten to handle those students for him and get him removed from his job. Such a situation can arise in small or rural or southern communities. But, then, in these communities, one is not likely to find too many radicals of either color in the community college.

There is a problem here for the black administrator. Whereas the white administrator can move into the militant groups by either their initiative or his own, black administrators are not likely to be invited to the meetings of groups on the far right. These groups do not permit him to hear what they are saying at the coffee break. While the black militants and white radicals say freely how they feel and what they think to the administrator regardless of his race, the conservative students on the right are tangential, oblique, and indirect as they deal with the black administrator. They circumvent him and go to whites on the staff to get information or to initiate a protest. They work through political representatives, advisory committees, unions, and other such groups. These students are concerned about what the black administrator has, what he wears, and how much power and influence he can use. Whereas blacks and white radicals threaten the black administrator with force, those on the right threaten him with lawyers and official and quasi-official actions, even though they have more means for force than the more activist students do.

Contrary to what is generally thought, these conservative students make more demands than do the radical students, even though the conservatives are not as vocal in their demands. They are not willing to openly confront the administrator so others can see what they want and do; rather, they attempt to apply pressure indirectly.

They can cause many problems for the administrator when they offer to take the law into their own hands. During confrontations, they may bring firearms to class with them. They are sometimes especially eager to prevent the activist students from flying the flag at half-staff and committing other "violations," although

43

this attitude is more prevalent in small rural and suburban colleges than in large urban ones.

There is usually little hope of bringing the extreme students on both sides together in a positive way during confrontation. No way. They can be brought together, however, during the lulls between confrontations, and they can be convinced that they should meet and discuss the problems on the campus and to listen to each other.

An administrator can also take some steps to minimize confrontation and the threat of confrontation among students. These steps require the attention of and coordination among many agencies and people. The administrator should get acquainted with the local newspaper reporter(s) who handles the educational news. At a meeting or several meetings, he must make it perfectly clear that he will be open and honest with the press and request the same commitment from the press. He should not attempt to hide the news when it is not favorable but should call the newspaper when trouble is brewing and ask the writer to come and see for himself. Such a course is preferable to having the reporter's contacts (found on every campus) call him and give information that is out of context or is incorrect or to having the group which is staging a demonstration give information or pass out press releases or call a press conference under the auspices of the college. Most reporters exercise good judgment when they find the administrator keeps his word. The administrator will find that what was getting front-page attention is buried farther and farther in the back of the paper, that the length of articles is getting shorter, and that the articles are balanced rather than sensational.

The next group that the administrator should invite in may well be the police. He must seek an agreement with the law enforcement agencies that no uniformed officers or officers in riot dress will appear at the campus unless they are called. This agreement does not preclude plainclothes officers from being in a crowd and otherwise available. The administrator must understand however that the police do not have to have his permission to come onto the campus. He is simply making a gentlemen's agreement with the police authorities to cooperate with him, and he must usually agree that he will assist in the identification of students if arrests are made. The school security system, other administrators, and the public information people should be coordinated with the city police force, and they must be in touch with each other when a confrontation seems imminent. A specific person should be designated to call the police when such an action is necessary. In his absence, another, and so on. This person should use code numbers so that demonstrators cannot call in law enforcement officers and make them one of the tools of the confrontation.

On-campus personnel must also be prepared for confrontation. Secretaries should be taught not to panic when there is a bomb threat or some other problem that can cause disruption on the campus. Handling such threats should be a well worked out process. In addition, every administrator on the staff should have a specific job if and when a confrontation arises. One should deal with the faculty, one with the students, and so forth. Even though faculty persuasions run the gamut from extreme right to extreme left, the administrator who deals with the faculty should get their assistance if he can. Sometimes it is also important to get faculty out of the way for their own safety. And sometimes it is necessary to tell them to mind their own damn business if they are attempting to mind the administrator's.

Another step in the process is to place hot lines in the offices of the most militant groups on campus since immediate telephone contact between the administrative offices and certain specific student groups is invaluable. Often, with a telephone call, the administrator can stop a damaging rumor which can lead to difficulty. (The chief administrator should also provide the police, fire department, and other sensitive and essential agencies his private number for the same reason.) The following case illustrates how valuable this hot line can be. An instructor at a West Coast community college called the security officer and related that a young black woman with a revolver had come prior to the beginning of his class looking for another woman. The officer left immediately for the class. Meanwhile, from a window the woman with the gun watched as the other woman and her husband drove into the parking lot. As she started out the door with the gun to confront the other woman, she met the security officer coming in. He delayed her and subsequently disarmed her. In the process, the revolver discharged. When the police arrived they had to restrain the woman, who had been disarmed, and almost drag her out of the building to the patrol wagon in full view of hundreds of students. As soon as the administrator heard of the incident, he called the leader of the Black Student Union and explained what had happened. Then he and the BSU leader provided immediate, accurate information in a joint communique to the rest of the staff and students. Both walked through the campus together and passed out the handbills within twenty minutes of the incident. Both the administrator and the activist student called the daily newspapers, jointly gave them the story, and elicited their cooperation in conveying the facts if they decided to run the story. The BSU man thanked the administrator for having a hot line so that they had contact, and the administrator thanked the student for helping him cool what could have been an explosive situation. The success in this situation is attributable to the availability of immediate communication. The cost of that telephone was not a hundred dollars a year. It probably saved several thousands of dollars, many subsequent problems with the community, and perhaps even lives.

Still another step in preventing confrontation is accessibility. For example, one college president concerned with his visibility to the students holds a rap session each week at different locations in the college. He has discovered that many students do not know the president of the college. At these sessions nothing is sacred. They are open forums with no holds barred. He wins a few arguments, loses a few. In either case, he makes himself available so students can get to him, see his strength, appreciate his weaknesses, watch him squirm or boast or both. In short, they see the human side of the man. He visits at least two buildings in the complex each day. He allows himself to be interrupted during any meeting with deans and others to listen to the problems of students. The whole administrative staff encourages students to come in at any time that suits their schedules. Visibility and availability can be maintained in many ways. Pictures of administrators should make up a rogues' gallery in every building or branch with short copy underneath to tell who each one is, what he does, where he can be found on campus, his telephone number, and so forth. Administrators, including the president, should make it a point to eat lunch in the student cafeteria several times each week and to table hop. The whole administrative staff should attend athletic events, drama productions, exhibits, political rallies, and all the other functions taking place in the college. The students soon learn who is available to them and who is not; who is interested in what they are doing and who ignores them; who shows up at commencement exercises and who does not; who can be found to talk to on the athletic field when the teaching staff is gone; who is willing to shoot a few baskets or play a set of tennis, a round of golf, a game of chess, or just sit around once in awhile and shoot the bull about politics.

When students know who their administrators are, where they can be found, what the parameters of their jobs are, what the limits of their authority are, who is responsible for what, they do not strike out blindly or attack because they know these people well. It has always been easier to attack an administrator than a faculty member, an office than a campus, a front man than those who put the administrator out front. By providing the students with the documents which delineate the authority he has, the administrator can take the proverbial monkey off his back and help the students to more accurately place it where it belongs—wherever that might be.

Another new constituency the community college administrator can expect to encounter is the Women's Liberation Movement. For several reasons this movement is significant to the community college. One reason is that Women's Lib sponsors day care, and day care is one of the growing issues in the community college. There is support for it everywhere. The President has proposed that day care facilities be greatly expanded so that welfare mothers can go to work. Some of these mothers also want to go to school.

The greatest need in the economy today is for persons with

47

technical skills; and every opportunity must be provided at the community college level to train or retrain persons to fill the needs of business and industry. The community college serves many low-income, federally assisted students who are single parents trying to acquire such salable skills in order to become self-sufficient. The mean student age in large, urban community colleges is twenty-five; many of these students have children under six years of age. The absence of day care facilities is a deterrent for many of these students who wish to attend the community college.

If they wish to avoid loss of time from class, students with children do not have many alternatives. Some occasionally bring children to the college. The classroom is neither a convenient nor a safe place for a child. His presence is distracting to other students and is often dismaying to staff, and being in a classroom can be hazardous to the child's health. Many other young children are left home, attended by older siblings (eight or nine years old) who are themselves truant. Others are left unattended while parents go to school or work.

Whether day care is the responsibility of the college is not the fundamental question for the administrator. That question is ultimately determined by the board of trustees, the legislature of the state, and so forth. The central question is: What does the administrator do when demands for day care are made? What is his recourse when students bring their young children to class and refuse to leave when the professor asks them to? One of the first things that the administrator should do is to provide those who are interested in day care with information concerning the funding source. They should know where college funds are expended, how, for what, which laws are applicable, and what the consequences are for those who do not spend the funds for the goods or services for which they are allocated. But even before the administrator makes this revelation, he should go on record supporting or rejecting the need for day care as an on-going function of the community college. If the administrator is against it, he should, nevertheless, provide all the available materials, meet with the students, ask his business manager and others who would be directly involved in such a program to assist, and use his influence to call in community people who may have both interest and expertise in the area. He should be willing to carry all requests to the board of trustees or to anyone else the students designate. If he is not willing to do these things, he should say so to the students, but then he should not, in any way, obstruct the students' attempts to exercise their own initiatives and prerogatives.

When a professor demands that a student not bring a young child into his classroom, it is not often feasible, wise, or good public relations to try to forcibly remove the student or the child. The other students in the class can usually handle the case best. The administrator's job is to convince the professor to be patient. These cases rarely last more than a few days because the parent is as embarrassed and inconvenienced as are the professor and the other students.

Women's Lib members maintain that day care is more important and serves more needs of more students than do football, basketball, track, and some other extracurricular activities which take a significant amount of the funds of an institution, exclude the female student for the most part, and, in large urban community colleges, attract only a very small segment of the student body. The community college administrator has a rather difficult time trying to refute their arguments. If such a venture is undertaken by the college, the necessary funds have to be appropriated regardless of the cost. Certain codes (fire, health, building) must be followed; insurance must be provided. When they are not, child care centers cannot operate.

Women's Lib is significant in community colleges for another reason. The women state that fewer women than men get jobs in the two-year college and that those who do are rarely elevated to top administrative positions such as president and dean. Only a few move into the lesser administrative jobs of division chairman and department head. Even with the same qualifications, women are not initially hired at the same rank as their male counterparts. One woman English instructor in Texas puts it this way:

49

Blind Man on a Freeway

We are always good enough to be assistants and do all of the work, but we are never good enough to be in charge. I work with men every day; and the truth is that many of them are carried by their assistants and especially their secretaries. I'll admit that we are a little better off than women in the university, but we're treated worse than the proverbial nigger. We want to be promoted commensurate with our abilities. Fortunately, the archaic system of giving everybody the same pay who has been on the job the same length of time provides us with equal pay. Believe me, some of the men here are overpaid. Why are American men so insecure? They laugh at us when we say we want to be equal; they treat us like children, define our roles, and ignore us except as sex partners. Yet, when we look at what these bungling jackasses have done to education in America, we have one consolation. The women didn't do it. I have never really known what a nigger is—I have only known who we were talking about—but, if he is treated like women in education are treated, I know how he feels and why he must be angry.

The teacher is correct. Women in education have not been treated fairly, especially in administration. Something can be done about it. The administrator can encourage women to apply when positions in administration and other responsible jobs are available. He can discriminate against male candidates in order to get females into administrative positions in his college or division in the same way he discriminated against women to keep them out of administration in the institution. He can provide on-the-job training for good female administrative prospects on his staff long before a vacancy arises. When a vacancy does occur and if the trainee has the qualifications, she can then be promoted to the position. The administrator can go out and specifically look for women who are equally as well qualified as their male counterparts. The American Council on Education, through its Academic Administration Intern Programs, is able not only to locate women candidates but also to encourage the institutions where they are assigned to grant them release time and to pay their salaries while they are doing the intern-

50

ship. Well trained women are available. They are not as hard to find as some say "qualified" blacks are.

Minority group students are another constituency to whom most community colleges have failed to give adequate consideration. One reason is that this constituency is associated with unusual controversy and unmatched urgency in the spectrum of issues confronting today's college administrators (Altman and Snyder, 1971, p. vii). Few minority students were enrolled in these institutions in the past. But now, spawned out of the crippling schools of big city ghettoes, from the farms, and from the reservations across the nation, minority students who are now enrolled in higher education, especially in the community college, have increased greatly in numbers. In some community colleges 40 to 50 per cent of the student body is minority students. Highland Park, San Antonio, East Los Angeles City College, and Compton College are examples (Carnegie Commission on Higher Education, 1970). There are more minority students in community colleges than in four-year institutions because of the lower cost and because of the lower standards for admission. By attending a two-year college, these students can hold a job at the same time, can live at home, and can learn a skill or vocation they can use in two years.

These students are also in college because the minority taxpayer is beginning to ask why his son is excluded from college when the college does not exclude his dollars from the budget. He is insisting that his son be educated at his level of ability, whatever that level happens to be. He is right. He is pointing out that the community college cannot shirk its responsibility to educate a certain segment because that segment is more difficult to educate than others. If the two-year school chooses this course, then the minority taxpayer promises to vote against all tax levies for education in the future.

Minority people are also taking a look at the so-called democratic institution that has few, if any, of their members among its faculty or counseling and administrative staff. They are looking at the recruiters from these colleges who seldom, if ever, recruit from minority communities. The perennial excuse is that "qualified" candidates cannot be found among nonwhites. Although no one seems to know what *qualified* means in educational selection (Birenbaum, 1971, p. 5), minority group members have effectively been denied access to higher education because of various definitions of quality (Kitano and Miller, 1970, p. i). Paradoxically, "the higher-educated have a worse record than the poorly educated at every occupational level—more absenteeism, turnover, dissatisfaction, and probably lower productivity" (Miller, 1967). Minority groups hear the humanities and the social studies faculties maintain that they are libertarians and hold equalitarian beliefs. They see, however, that these same faculties do not choose as their teaching colleagues members from minority groups. Minority group students resent administrators who permit teachers to use research which appears to be racist, such as that of Jensen (1969), as a basis for not admitting them into the college, particularly since his work has been refuted by many. The students are watching the administrators who never come to their communities to speak. They are noting that displays from the college are in other parts of the city and never in their own.

Discrimination is also evident in the educational program of the college. Some apprenticeship, vocational, and technical programs do not have a single minority group member enrolled. Division chairmen and instructors in some vocational areas ask to see students before they accept them into classes. In one community college dental hygiene program, all the girl students were natural blonds and had about the same physical proportions and blue eyes. No student without those characteristics was ever admitted. When confronted with this fact, the department head indicated to the division chairman, the dean of instruction, and the college president that they were interfering with her academic freedom. She continued by saying that no patient in the dentists' offices that the school served would want the hands of a black hygienist in his mouth; no dentist would accept "the sloppy habits of a Mexican in his office." Contact with the dental offices served by the school revealed that in all but one office the dentist has asked for assistants other than blonds; one dentist was embarrassed that every female in his office was blond.

New Students, New Faculty, New Demands

Another dentist had specifically asked for a black hygienist and had been told that no black girls applied for admission to the program. A search of applications on file turned up sixty-one applicants in a six-year period. Forty-two of them met all the qualifications except having blond hair, blue eyes, the right weight, although most of the applicants met the latter standard. Such discrimination, though not quite so blatant, can be found repeatedly. In many apprenticeship areas, unions with their notorious discrimination policies seem to have more influence on the curriculum than the college does. It should not be surprising, therefore, that many minority group people do not indicate that they would like to go into the vocational program. They would rather play it safe in the traditional areas of teaching, medicine, and law, even when the possibility of their completing such programs is remote.

Minority students who have been subjected to no teaching, poor teaching, many failures, and personal debasement in ghetto high schools will not subject themselves to the same abuse in college because they are older and determine their own behavior and because some are financially independent. There is also a movement toward the development of the use of arrogance by minority students as a technique for handling educators. They hold their heads high. These minority group students in junior colleges approach and respond to higher education differently from white and from minority students in large four-year colleges. The majority of those in four-year institutions are middle-class youth who have not encountered the poverty cycle, cultural deprivation, and academic failure which the students from the ghettos and the rural communities know well. They have many of the assets that any college student has. As a consequence, they are amenable to trying negotiation, discussion, "proper" and paper channels before they act. They know what is due them and have the intelligence and sensitivity to create confrontation with far-reaching effects, especially since they can demonstrate and document the condition which perpetrates their actions. Disadvantaged minority students are from a different class and respond with different behavior. They tend to respond to frustration with aggression instead of discussion.

53

Blind Man on a Freeway

The two-year college must come to terms with the fact that it is dealing with a new minority student, a student who is imbued with militancy. He has been hostile to the education process because that process has never provided for his needs, and he expects the community college to be one more part of a system that will not help him. He has heard all the arguments about poor homes, low cultural standards, and inferior life styles of the community where he lives. This student is now holding his head high, however, stressing his own culture and values, demanding that the books and other resources that he uses in the institution reflect some of these values and this culture. Consequently, he wants to have some say when his teacher is chosen. He also feels free to criticize the teacher's method of instruction and to let the college know it should do more than it is to adapt to his life style. In short, this new minority student no longer feels beyond redemption the way many—especially those in the educational system—have led him to believe he is.

The college must respond to this new militancy in two ways. It must give special attention to the way each minority student (black, Chicano, Native American, Puerto Rican, Oriental) differs from the traditional college student, for whom the present system of higher education is planned. And, at the same time, it must provide for the learning difficulties of this student as it provides for the learning abilities of honor students.

Regarding the first requirement, if college people are to be effective in dealing with the student who is culturally different, they should know his habits, behaviors, and attitudes. Many of these characteristics are never documented, although they are likely to be quite different from those of white students. The minority student is more cynical than the white because of what the system has done to him. He does not always believe in God, Mother, Country, and the other eternal and immutable values with the same fervor as does his white counterpart or his own parents. He is blunt, direct, candid, not given to little charades; if he does not like the teacher, he does not pretend to like him. His heroes are few; he does not trust the heroes that society creates, believing they must have feet of clay. He can take disappointments better than middle-class white students because in his world disappointment is a way of life. The minority student is more worldly than the white student, though he is often less sophisticated academically. His ingenuity is demonstrated outside of the classroom. Inside the traditional classroom he is more of a spectator than a participant. He considers as trivia the bits and pieces of knowledge which middle-class students use to show off with. The minority student has always been more tolerant of injustice, stupidity, sarcasm, dirt, profanity, and illegitimacy than the white student. He listens to and associates with students whom faculty members and administrators do not consider good students or good citizens because he views these individuals as real, honest, and candid people. In addition, the minority student does not confide in his parents and is unwilling to let a teacher or another arbiter handle problems or confrontation between himself and others. He has been independent too long for that, and he has had to solve his own problems and often bear his own misfortunes without assistance or sympathy. Many minority students, especially those with ghetto and migratory backgrounds, have been on their own since early childhood.

The problems encountered in meeting the second requirement—providing for the learning of minority students—are staggering to the imagination. Many of these problems have to do with their poor previous academic performances, as I point out elsewhere (Moore, 1970a):

> It is a fair statement that the marginal students are deficient in the traditional language arts (reading, writing, listening, spelling, speaking, grammar) and mathematics. The average high-risk student, after more than a decade of experience in the elementary and secondary schools, has not mastered these skills. He cannot read well enough to handle the traditional complexities of college bibliographies. He has not come to terms with the comprehensive and manipulatory skills in mathematics. And he has a blind spot when he is requested to write a theme or term paper. In fact, in the area of English, the high-risk student becomes immediately confused in the academic cross-breeding of intransitive verbs, direct objects, and

possessive pronouns. The failure of the marginal student to master the basic skills has added frustration to his many past semesters of discontent. This failure has also provided his teachers with evidence which they have used to judge the student as academically incompetent. The improvement of basic skills, then, should be a part of any curriculum for the academically slow student. These skills are fundamental. They are prerequisites to most learning in the formal classroom. Mastery of them will open the door to many intellectual, vocational, and economic alternatives. Without them, few opportunities are available.

Not infrequently the minority student wants teachers from his own group to tutor him. If those instructors are too rigorous, he may want them replaced. Most teachers in the community college do not want to instruct him at all—not so much because he is a minority group member, although this is a factor, as because he is often academically slow. They do not have the skills necessary to give instruction to this student; frequently they know absolutely nothing about his culture and show little or no desire to learn about it as an aid in providing adequate instruction. It takes time to deal with the learning problems of minority students. They require attention that goes beyond that normally given to freshman and sophomore students whose admission to college has been on a select basis. Special adjustment and adaptation are needed in both the instructing process and the material used. Minority students are often thought of as disadvantaged students. Many of them are, in various ways, disadvantaged. This adds to the problems of the instructors. In Chapter Three the entire discussion is on the educationally disadvantaged student. Thus, discussion of the problems of instruction and of teacher interaction with the students is omitted here.

Let us now turn to some specific gripes of minority students and ways administrators can alleviate the problems they indicate. Perhaps the problem that minority students talk about most is how members of their group have been excluded from acceptance by the community in general and from most of the opportunities and rewards of higher education in particular. When minority students enroll in an institution, they know that the traditional education is antiminority (Gibson, 1970, p. 13). Their images are not in the texts used to educate them. Their values are tolerated rather than appreciated; their life style is condemned. The contributions of their groups are never mentioned or applauded. Their heroes are never honored. In fact, they have been systematically excluded from the college by admissions criteria, quotas, discrimination, and all the other traditional exclusionary tactics which minority groups label institutional racism.

That institutional racism is clearly seen in other ways. It is seen in the college's predominantly all-white staffing pattern, in the observable racist attitude and behavior on the part of some of that staff, in the hypocrisy of liberal rhetoric but conservative action; and it is seen unmistakably in the insistence that the educative process continue in the elitist and racist tradition of its European origin. All these things militate to keep certain people out of the college. This exclusion cannot happen without the knowledge and confirmation of the administration. Neither individual nor institutional bigotry can operate in an institution for any sustained period of time without the knowledge of the administrator. There is little doubt that the teaching of young Americans, the administering of educational institutions, and the development of educational philosophy, curricula, and program are still largely white man's work. Despite government-imposed quotas, timetables, and other requirements which accompany some financial grants and aid to institutions, despite some voluntary in-house attempts at solutions, despite some outreach programs to recruit minorities, and despite seemingly constant litigation, the number of minority workers entering the community college as teachers and administrators remains a trickle. The administrator cannot plead alienation from or ignorance of the situation. At some point, regrettably, one must conclude that the absence of minorities in top-level positions in community colleges is no accident. Their exclusion is the result of purposeful discrimination. Sometimes the discrimination is subtle; sometimes it is not. It has been so much a way of life and such an integral part of the higher education bureaucracy that it seems unconscious. Few would deny that it is

57

axiomatic for bureaucracies to fight to prevent change, even when the prevailing situation is wrong.

Outspoken tell-it-like-it-is bigotry is rare these days. Today it is manifested in shortsightedness, snobbishness, narrow vision, insensitivity, hackneyed cliches, fabrications accepted as truth, and questionable research. Too many administrators are themselves the couriers and the people who have kept minorities out of higher education. Even when administrators want to change a situation, they resist calling attention to the existence of bigotry in their institutions. A considerable number of them attempt to manage the bigotry charges which reach their attention by placating and isolating the victim so that he will not create too much of a problem. They may convince the guilty instructor or administrator that he should apologize to the student. At other times, they treat the student as the villain rather than the victim. It is because minority group students are aware that administrators know of these conditions in the college and do absolutely nothing about them that they hold him in such contempt. When the bitterness of the past is catapulted into the present and manifested in campus riots and other student actions and demands, the administrator gets to be the heavy in a drama that is not of his choosing and he has to play the part despite the fact that he may not have adequate skills and preparation for doing so.

Minority students have other specific gripes about the administration. They insist that administrators are masters of evasion because they rarely, if ever, give a student a direct answer to his question. And the answers that they do provide are suspect. This suspicion is not without some basis. Students say, for example, that administrators attempt to talk them out of their grievances, especially when the complaint is against a faculty member. They note that when an administrator agrees to listen to a specific student's grievance, he immediately pulls the student's record, checks his grades, and evaluates his academic and deportment history and his attendance pattern. Thus, the student has to insist that his grievance gets reviewed in the first place and then has to have his credibility established before the administrator takes action. Moreover, the students expect the action taken to be only further delaying tactics because administrators are too fearful of faculty reactions. They want to know how the faculty will respond before they act. So they often give student grievances and issues to faculty senates and other such bodies, which frequently play parliamentary games with them. Students have come to expect this latter procedure as a typical administrative maneuver. And they are no longer willing to submit to the deliberations of such assemblies, which do not have a history of providing very many enlightened answers on anything, may not reach a decision on their issue, have not established any precedent for rulings which protect the rights of students. And the assembly itself often provides nothing more than an exercise in the democratic process for the participants and an opportunity for a skillful parliamentarian to obstruct all activity, using as his vehicle the rules of order.

The students gripe because administrators accept the widespread assumption and belief that acceptance of high-risk students lowers an institution's standards and somehow reduces its quality of education. This is far from the truth because these students, like all students, must meet the same requirements to progress (Nunez, 1971, p. 135). Nonwhite students claim that financial aid officers have little or no interest in the financial problems of poor and disadvantaged students (Baker, 1971, p. 149). George Nash of Columbia University's Bureau of Applied Social Research, in a speech at the College Scholarship Service Colloquium in Scottsdale, Arizona, was most direct as he corroborated, with evidence, the above claim.

There are many other gripes that the administrator should know about. He can also be sensitive to the needs of minority students by being aware of the language he uses as he talks with them. The student he called a Mexican American when he was attempting to be polite a decade ago no longer accepts that name. He now prefers to be called Chicano. Those students who were called Indians now prefer to be called by the name that more accurately describes who they are, Native Americans. The group which struggled for generations to legitimatize the term Negro now wishes to be called black. New labels are good signs among minority groups; they are a new source of pride. Whites, however, are not quite ready for these changes in terms, which is understandable since they did not generate the terms. In the past, whites determined what other people would be called. Now the people decide themselves what they choose to be called. After a black speaker's presentation at a workshop, a member of the audience asked, "Why do you want to be called black? You're not black."

"You're not white."

"I never thought of that."

"That's the problem."

The importance of being familiar with new labels is emphasized by this illustration: A financial aids officer in a two-year college received a telephone call from two students requesting information concerning a loan. Because the officer could detect an accent, he asked the students to identify themselves. When the students said they were Chicanos, the officer informed them that "this office does not provide loans for 'foreign' students. That function is performed by another officer." This statement by the financial aids officer was all that was needed to trigger a confrontation. Newspapers were called; Chicano students from a nearby university came to the campus to protest and demonstrate. The university student newspaper picked up the story and ran banner headlines about the incident. The rest of this type of story is now cliche. The man who did not know that the word *Chicano* designated an American-born individual of Mexican descent was, in fact, a very fine man who enjoyed an excellent reputation with the students. He did much of his graduate study in the area of minority groups. His problem was that he spent so much of his time studying about minorities that he had failed to continue listening to them and to keep abreast of what was going on. Had he listened and been more sensitive he would be aware that there is a dynamic vernacular used by minority group students and that best known among them is the vernacular used by blacks. If he had been a black administrator he would have learned the slang and other colloquial expressions for dealing with minority groups first.

The administrator who hopes to be able to communicate with minority groups has to spend some time learning what to say and not to say. Even the term *minority* is not palatable to many who do not hesitate to inform the speaker to use *nonwhite*. These students and others are more accurate in their use of language than are the educators who are supposed to have greater ability to verbalize. Those in academic ranks are not necessarily more creative, accurate, or colorful in their choice of terms. Minority group people certainly did not create the term *disadvantaged*.

Labor union groups in education are a final constituency. Since 1960, concomitant with the growth of the community college has been growth in the demands and gains of faculty through negotiations. Teacher unions and other associations consistently outmaneuver administrators and boards of trustees in the negotiation process. Administrators have proved to be no match for these bargaining groups because they develop no skill in and acquire no knowledge about the negotiation process in their training.

The one outstanding characteristic of teacher labor groups is that they are consistently more concerned about their own welfare than about education. Sidney P. Marland, Jr. (1971), commissioner of education, puts it this way: "No sound evidence has been offered by teacher organizations to demonstrate that improved circumstances for teachers have brought improved learning." In an accreditation report of a Northwest community college, the evaluators wrote, "Although the establishment of an exclusive bargaining agent . . . may be commendable, the committee noted great concern with wages, hours, and working conditions and little attention for quality in teaching and learning." Despite many published statements indicating vital concern with providing better service and education for the student, these organizations seem to provide more for themselves than for the students. It is naive to even think that bargaining is going to be done on behalf of the student. Salaries are getting higher; work loads are getting smaller; instructors are working shorter hours (since 1960 the average number of work days in community colleges has decreased by ten). There is more vacation leave; many schools allow personal leave; some community colleges grant sabbatical leave after two years. And teachers all over the country are asking for and winning the right to negotiate policy.

61

Blind Man on a Freeway

There is little doubt that improvement of welfare and other benefits for teachers has been greatly needed. Community college instructors, like other people, deserve as many benefits as they can accrue. They should be paid well for their services and should receive other benefits. But, along with these increased benefits, the education process should improve. Yet, by any criteria the reader may wish to apply, the education of the student is not getting better; it is getting worse. The student is not getting more attention, time, or service, or better instruction as a result of better teacher welfare and benefits.

In addition to noting the apparent well deserved fringe benefits earned by unions (or other bargaining agents) for their members, one must also observe and record the kind of behavior exhibited by some of those members. Much of this behavior is unprofessional, if not unethical. The other members, through their silence, permit unethical and unprofessional activities to take place at the expense of the students they serve. If these observations seem unfair, the reader and the administrator have but to make some basic observations of and ask some basic questions about the behavior of teachers who are members of bargaining groups: Are the instructors who are most concerned about bargaining and teacher welfare among the most effective on the staff? Are they among the tutors who are always willing to advise students? Are they the volunteers who are willing to work with the disadvantaged, high-risk, and minority students, or do any outreach work? Are they the teachers who can be found on campus before nine or after two? Can students expect them to keep their office hours? Do they welcome accountability? Are they among the teachers who have done the most to improve instruction in the college? Are these instructors the most innovative and creative professionals on the staff? Are there fewer complaints from the students assigned to their classes than from those in the classes of other instructors on campus? Do the letters of praise commending individual teachers (which an administrator sometimes receives) also include them? These are fair questions.

There is no attempt to say here that all teachers who are members of bargaining groups do not have the positive qualities implied by the above questions. The fact remains, however, that the items bargained for in contracts indicate that the concerns and needs of students are not the primary—or even secondary—concerns of instructors in bargaining groups. The teacher demands which follow illustrate this point (only four examples are included here). One group stated one such demand in this way:

It is acknowledged that duly elected officers of the bargaining agent may be required to spend additional time in executing provisions of this agreement. Accordingly, the following schedules of "release time" will be maintained: (1) The bargaining agent president for the year will be given up to one-half teaching load off for the winter, spring, and fall quarters. He will receive full pay during this time. (2) In addition, four other bargaining agent members who are designated as part of the bargaining agent's negotiations team will be given full pay and a two-thirds work load during spring quarter, provided that their names are submitted in writing to the administration no later than February 1, and assuming that contract negotiations will take place in spring quarter.

Does the foregoing demand provide for the needs of students, improve instruction or the institution, or make any other contribution to the educational process? Why should a board of trustees, a president, or other negotiators agree to such a demand? The administrative team of the community college where this demand was made granted it. This team did not protect the students, the public, or the other faculty members. The extra cost inevitably is taken from instruction, equipment, and other educational services. But even more to the point, why should an institution pay an agent to work against it and the public it is supposed to serve?

Another community college group of faculty negotiators demanded that the daily instructional work span not exceed five hours and, during that time, provision be made for a luncheon break, student conferences, and other assigned professional duties. The demand further established the following limitations:

Blind Man on a Freeway

*(1) Nothing in this section shall be construed to mean that:
(a) the teaching span is five hours in length; or (b) faculty members are expected to be on campus for this total span. (2) No split shifts will be scheduled unless specifically requested in writing by the faculty member prior to the beginning of the quarter.*

The stated reason for this demand was that faculty members needed the extra time for preparation. Administrators, students, and others are well aware of this great preparation myth. There is, to be sure, a need to prepare good material, and it takes time. The question is, Does it take as much time as is demanded? When the editor of the student newspaper of this particular community college later saw this demand printed in the negotiated agreement, he wrote an editorial.

Teachers are not the only professionals who need preparation time. Most professionals take work home, "burn the midnight oil," and keep abreast of what is going on in their fields, without reduction in their work loads or hours. It is a fact that those who are in community college instruction actually have more time to prepare than workers in most other professions. They have extended vacations at Christmas and Easter time, during semester and/or quarter breaks, and an eight- to eleven-week vacation in summer. Their salaries are based on an academic year of nine months, or between 165 to 185 instruction days. They work fifty to sixty days less than most other workers—professional or otherwise. Other workers are not provided with, nor do they expect, extra salary and other inducements to get them to do what any professional is expected to do. An eight-hour day is the normal work time on most jobs. We do not say that an instructor in the community college must necessarily work an eight-hour day or that an institution should not provide good benefits for the professional personnel. What this newspaper is saying is the man on the street and every student on campus should question the need for so much extra time and extra pay that college people say is necessary to prepare them to do what they al-

ready claim to be experts at doing. Elementary and high school teachers do not get this extra time for planning and they work longer hours, deal with more students, have more clerical chores to perform, work more instruction days each year, do not choose the students they want to teach, and the overwhelming majority of them have the same academic qualifications as community college instructors. Primary teachers work even harder; in the beginning grades they start with illiterates. It would seem that teaching illiterates would require more preparation time than giving instruction to young adults.

If a man needs as much time to prepare to give instruction to his students in each succeeding year as he needed the preceding year, either he is a slow learner, he is teaching a different course, or his subject matter revolutionizes each year. Let's face it, it is less than professional for a group of people to force an institution with the threat of strike or some like alternative to guarantee them additional welfare, educational, and other personal benefits which will guarantee nothing in return—neither improvement in instruction, service to the student, nor, in most cases, professional improvement in themselves. The student and the taxpayer have a right to expect these latter guarantees. Administrators are aware of this. Yet, they do little or nothing to change the situation. They are, in fact, the people who agree to many of the demands without following the implications of such demands to their logical conclusion and consequences for you the student. How many times have you watched your professor lecture from the same yellowing, frayed notes? How many times have you gotten a copy of an old exam and found that the professor has not even changed the arrangement of the questions? How many classes have you attended where the professor did not bother to cover up the fact that he is not prepared? Why can't students send representatives to the bargaining table along with the faculty and administrators? Somebody should be available to protect the student. Students are what all of this is about in the first place, aren't they? The professors who scream loudest and most often about needing more time to prepare are the ones we see teaching all of the *extra night courses; because of their seniority they get the first opportunity to teach summer courses; and they are also the ones who seem to have the poorest preparation. Perhaps if they were less greedy and were not trying to make every extra buck by working nights and summers, they would have time to prepare. This paper has just been informed that the average salary is $12,260 for nine months' work, exclusive of night work and summer work. Adding these latter two work periods, an instructor at the maximum salary can go up to an additional $5,000. Some instructors in this college earn $20,000 and more. Great! But they should prepare on their own time.*

In a third community college, the bargaining agent wrote this clause into the agreement with the board of trustees:

The board and the bargaining agent agree that the system can most effectively meet the changing needs of today's society by involving students, faculty, administration, and members of the community in the planning and governance of the institution. The following policies will apply: (1) Effective immediately the board will add a faculty member in a nonvoting capacity to its membership. This faculty member will be eligible to attend all meetings— public and executive—except when the board determines that a private discussion on a sensitive matter is desirable. (2) The faculty member who acts in this capacity will serve for a minimum of one year and will receive in-service credits, as prescribed by the director of instructional personnel, for such service.

The bargaining agent which proposed the above agreement voted against every attempt to involve a broad spectrum of the community once this item in the proposal was granted. It rejected the administration's proposal for a senate-council representing everyone in the college community (students, faculty, administration, and classified personnel). The bargaining unit gave the following reasons for its action: (1) The bargaining unit can perform the functions. (2) There is not sufficient information as to the functions, authority, and structure of the proposed senate. (3) It is an abdication of administrative responsibilities. (4) It is not the best use of faculty, student, and administrative time. (5) Current committee structure, augmented by student participation, provides a better means of dealing with concerns. (6) The logistics, in terms of group size and meeting times, are bad. The real reason was that this group considered the governance body a threat to them.

A fourth proposal, this time with regard to counselors, read: "The counselor's 175-day contract shall cover *only the period within the regular instructional year, as prescribed by the applicable school calendar;* i.e., fall quarter, winter quarter, spring quarter." Counselors are educational specialists. Much of their work is done outside the school calendar. Counselors should expect to work during the summer, between quarters, and during other periods when college is not in session. In short, their calendar is, or should be, different from the calendar of a classroom instructor. The above proposal guaranteed extra pay for every time the counselor served his function when school was not in session. Agreeing to this work assignment was neither administratively nor educationally sound.

There is little point to offering more examples. The point should be clear. It was only important to show the extent to which demands almost completely ignore the student. The table of contents for a proposed Michigan Association of Higher Education agreement, 1968–1969, contained over two hundred specific items in eleven categories, including association and instructors' rights, deductions for professional dues, conditions of employment, basic class loads and overloads, course preparation, office hours, attendance at college functions, teaching facilities, faculty facilities, faculty parking, academic freedom, meetings, interview expenses, moving expenses. More than 95 per cent of the items had absolutely nothing to do with the improvement of instruction, service to the student, or professional improvement.

The administrator's primary concern in dealing with these demands is not what benefits faculty can accrue but rather that the student not be denied his rights. The administrator should guarantee that the faculty has its rights and privileges granted and protected, as well as extending and maintaining students' rights and privileges. He should be especially concerned with improving instruction and service to the whole institution and should expect that his rights will also be protected.

Most of the demands made by all groups in an institution fall into three categories—reasonable, illegal, and absurd. When an administrator is required to negotiate, he should keep some basic considerations in mind. He should know what the labor laws are and how they affect his institution, how to locate and retain advice and guidance from a competent consultant, how to select an attorney with the needed expertise in labor law, how to determine whether a demand is educationally sound and at the same time lawful, and how to maintain flexibility within the institution by the agreements which he is making. Above all, the administrator must know that although he has to bargain, he does not have to make concessions or agree to proposals. In addition, the administrator must be aware of some common sense considerations: (1) The board of trustees and the administration will negotiate within the constraints of fiscal responsibility. (2) The board of trustees will agree only to that which is educationally sound and that which emphasizes the improvement of instruction. (3) The administration and board of trustees will not agree to that which abridges the rights of students. (4) The board of trustees and the administration will protect the rights of the public, their own rights, and the quality of the institution. (5) The board of trustees and the administration are committed to the philosophy of the open-door community college and will maintain that concept in theory and practice. (6) The board of trustees will maintain and preserve the authority of administrators commensurate with their responsibility. (7) The president's authority will not be vested in the faculty.

Organizations as well as individuals do not approve of much of the union activity. At least one national organization, the American Association of Higher Education, has severed relations with the National Education Association (NEA) because of its "militant collective bargaining mood" (Steif, 1971). The behavior of the larger organization (NEA) was considered irresponsible. Commissioner of Education Marland asserts: "Bargained gains for teachers, no matter how long overdue and justified, have been counterproductive thus far. There are two major issues arising from the shift of the teaching profession into the labor movement which might find their ultimate resolution in legislation. They are: (1) Some of the conventional practices of labor are not suited to the teaching profession; (2) the teacher now committed to a bargained arrangement with management must accept the economic consequences calling for productivity and accountability."

The bargaining constituency is a well organized and dedicated one. Long after students stop playing governance and many of them return to dating, football, employment, and marriage as their primary activities, after the militants have become respectable or have been repressed, after the women have been pacified with day care centers, after the minorities have been placated, and after attrition has claimed its masses, this bargaining constituency will still be around. Its demands will become past practices and tradition—replete with court decisions, arbitration boards, and all the other trappings of labor unions. It appears inevitable that the academic professional will become the educated tradesman—or worse. As these changes occur, the education of students will get worse. And it is almost a certainty that the improvement of instruction will come to a standstill. The tragedy is that the educator should know better.

Opening the Closed Door

The literature has been redundant since 1960 in describing the needs, behavior, and problems of the educationally disadvantaged in the community college. Knoell (1970), Morgan (1970), the Carnegie Commission on Higher Education (1970), and other researchers continue to document the need for quality post-high school education for disadvantaged students on the one hand and the way community college educators ignore these students on the other. Now administrators must face the facts. In 1965, more than 60 per cent of the students in the community college were at or below the thirtieth percentile on the SCAT. The Center for Research and Development in Higher Education determined that 49 per cent of the students enrolled in the community colleges of four states (California, Illinois, Massachusetts, North Carolina) were in the first and second quartiles. Except for those in a few community colleges tucked away in small suburban areas, these students are as I have described them in earlier writings (Moore, 1968a, 1968d, 1969, 1970a). While their numbers are rapidly increasing (they now constitute the largest segment of two-year college registrants), community colleges on the whole have failed to respond to them in a positive way.

The administrator needs to know what these students think and why, primarily because they are the students who give him difficulty. They are a large and diversified group consisting of minority group members, poor whites, and others. The most vocal and active among them are the blacks. In New York, Puerto Ricans are vocal and active also; on the West Coast, Chicanos are extremely militant. There has also been considerable activity among Orientals. The administrator should know who these people are, how they feel, and what they are saying. He should decide early what commitments he is willing to make to them and what assistance he can expect.

The many terms for this group—*culturally disadvantaged, culturally deprived, high-risk, inner- or core-city youth, ghetto students, the culturally different*—have been used interchangeably to describe students who manifest extreme deficiencies in physiological, psychological, and sociological areas which educators say are important for performing optimally in school and in the mainstream of society. Social class, race, limited or no previous educational tradition in the family, behavior different from that which had always been viewed as "acceptable," and the other well known accompaniments of poverty and degradation are characteristics which classify a person as *disadvantaged*. The problem is that educators have become addicts and, therefore, victims of the descriptive terms which completely confuse them, the lay community, and the persons labeled because they do not describe these students accurately.

When I use the term *disadvantaged* here, I am referring to a group which is using the community college as a service vehicle to achieve social, academic, vocational, financial, or personal satisfaction. The group may include students who traditionally would not be considered college students at all because of their erratic high school records, economic plight, unimpressive standardized test scores, and race/cultural/class distinctions. Some of the students

71

are illiterate and need basic education; some are foreign born and need only English as a second language proficiency; some are unwed, expectant mothers whom the public elementary and high schools have excluded; some are veterans who are barely functionally literate and who could not (and should not) be expected to continue their education in a high school or junior high school environment. Some have left the rigidity, stagnation, irrelevancy, tradition, and punitiveness of the public educational system and have been labeled *dropouts* by that system. Many have been pushed out by the system because it does not understand them and has not learned to educate them. Another group of these students has been pushed through the education system without positive significant change taking place either in the acquisition of skills and knowledge or in an acceptance of the "important" values that the educators have prescribed. Most of these students are white and poor. Although their numbers are smaller, those getting considerable attention are black and poor. Other minorities are also among the disadvantaged; they too are poor. They come from rural areas, from small ethnic enclaves, and from the teeming ghettos of our big cities. They are different primarily because they are void of the education, goods, services, and experiences provided for middle-class students. As a consequence, the positive attitudes and expectations which are the hallmarks of the middle-class students are lacking in disadvantaged students.

How do these students feel about the community college? The administrator should know that although these students are using the community college as a vehicle to achieve social, academic, vocational, financial, and some personal satisfaction, they believe that the education (and the people who educate) in this institution, like most post-high school education, stresses exclusiveness and elitism. And they know that students who are not white and primarily middle-class are not recruited by, wanted in, or welcomed into any significant number of community colleges. Students are aware of the general feeling of people in higher education that those who are described as being disadvantaged cannot make a contribution to the institution, enrich the lives and experiences of students who are middle-class, add to the knowledge of mankind, or profit from the educational venture themselves. Disadvantaged students constantly point out that no plans were made for them in post-high school education until recently. They resent the label disadvantaged, and they resent being studied. They call attention to the fact that in the open-door college, the curriculum is not as open as the doors.

Repeatedly, the students indicate that one reason why there have been so few opportunities for the disadvantaged is the lack of interest on the part of institutional leadership—primarily faculty leadership. They know that faculties are able to get most of the changes in an institution that they desire; and they know that their instructors are equally as effective in restricting important change if they choose to ignore the demand for it, feel threatened by it, or want to erect barriers to prevent it. Contrary to what is generally thought, lack of funds, inadequate space, too little know-how, and other generally accepted (but poorly examined) theses are not the main reasons why better education is not more accessible to the disadvantaged. Lack of faculty interest and leadership and a definite, though sometimes subtle, faculty resistance to change (with racist undertones) are perhaps the most significant reasons why we have seen so little real opportunity and so much inaction for the disadvantaged in higher education. This is as true in the community college as it is in other post-high school institutions; and the administrator should be well aware of this. Since 1960, students have been saying that most faculties have neither wanted nor attempted to understand and empathize with the disadvantaged and their world, particularly if that world is black. While the faculty leadership has not applied pressure from the bottom up, the administration has not attempted to exert strong leadership from the top down. The administrator must face the fact that programs for the disadvantaged do not have much support from professional educators above the high school level. It is, therefore, understandable why disadvantaged students are critical of both administrators and faculty. In the remainder of this chapter I summarize their frustrations as revealed to me in sixty "Rap with the President" sessions.

For the educationally disadvantaged, one of the administrator's most important tasks is improvement in the quality of instruction. Yet this job, when it is performed at all, takes place because of administrative default. Middle-class citizens and legislators, by defeating tax levies and by refusing to vote larger appropriations for education, respectively, now agree with the disadvantaged that administrators are unconvincing when they state that it takes only more money to provide a quality education. Disadvantaged students have been disagreeing with this simplistic argument since the beginning of the war on poverty in the sixties because it fails to get at the real problem of a quality education for the disadvantaged. Since the 1950s citizens have been supporting education at a much higher rate than they did in the previous one hundred years, and the quality of education has not improved for a significant and representative group of students. Both privileged and disadvantaged students also agree that administrators seem to have a brick and mortar passion. School managers want monuments of palatial splendor which have little, if anything, to do with quality education.

Administrators generally claim that with sufficient funds they can do wonderful things for community college education, including attracting and retaining top faculty and administrators. However, it is not now and never has been difficult to find teaching and administrative staff for the community college. There are more teaching applicants in all disciplines than there are positions to be filled, and one also does not find it difficult to locate administrative candidates.

It is more than money. Ask a dean of instruction or a division/department chairman whether instruction for the disadvantaged improves with increases in faculty-administrative salaries. Inquire of him whether sophisticated instructional equipment such as audiovisual aids and other learning resources has made any significant change and brought any improvement in the rate of learning or in the quantity, quality, and relevance of what students learn or whether the continuing increase in the number of counselors in the community college brings a corresponding decrease in the attrition rate of deprived and other students or an increase in the number of students who enroll. Ask the librarian whether a new library building replete with all the latest equipment and reference materials (to meet American Library Association standards) has improved education for the disadvantaged or even improved the book circulation for all the students in the college.

When the disadvantaged student comes to the college and receives minimum assistance, he encounters an oppressive system which frustrates him: rules and regulations, structure, the various hierarchies of faculty and administrative rank, and doctors who don't ever treat anybody. The system is too big, complex, and overwhelming for him to readily understand (Knoell, 1968; Cross, 1968; Moore, 1970a; Morgan, 1970). The student knows only that his teacher causes him concern. He is soon keenly aware that the faculty member is a significant person in an institution. In fact, the faculty member designs curricula, awards grades, decides what is to be taught, controls who is admitted by determining selection criteria, chooses his working hours and standards for promotion, ad infinitum. The relationship with this individual, academic and personal, turns the disadvantaged student on or off early.

There is no delicate way to say that disadvantaged students, especially minority students, do not like or trust their teachers (Clark, 1965; Silberman, 1964; Moore, 1969, 1970a; Riessman, 1962), and it would be a mere academic distraction to belabor the few exceptions. Educators, writers, community organizers, and others who work with disadvantaged students consistently emphasize the attitude of these students toward their teachers and the lack of respect and trust that they express toward their academic tutors. This lack of affection and trust starts early in the elementary grades. The feelings deepen, harden, and the students become increasingly embittered and inaccessible as they move through school. And, in talking to them, one finds an unmistakable consistency in the descriptions they give of the attitudes and the behavior of teachers toward them. Perhaps in every case, the students' charges cannot be objectively substantiated. Nonetheless, feelings are real. Disadvantaged students in the community college are extremely sensitive to the behavior of their instructors because most of them have a history of failure and humiliation at their hands.

75

Blind Man on a Freeway

One of the specific reasons for the anger of educationally disadvantaged students toward their teachers is the reliance of the teachers on cultural deprivation theories. These students reject the idea that they do not succeed in school because there were few or no books or newspapers in their homes or because their fathers did not sit at the dinner table and discuss world problems or take them to the zoo when they were young children. They reject the proposal that they are not able to succeed in school because some of their moral, spiritual, and social values are different; they reject the idea that they are inherently inferior (what some have come to call Jensenism) (Gordon, 1969), and finally, they reject blaming the student for the ineffective instruction—thus making him both the villain and the victim. These rejected reasons are tenets of the cultural deprivation theory. Riessman (1962) and Deutsch (1962) have formulated and supported much of this theory almost to the exclusion of other considerations. Hightower (1970), although writing about art, dispels it:

We hear much about "quality" and "standards" when suggestions are made for altering accepted credentials for academic acceptance or artistic excellence. We also hear much about "cultural deprivation," which means, of course, that people in [some minority group] neighborhoods do not hear white symphonies or see white plays; and it implies that the culture of the ghetto is primitive compared to white culture. Yet, the black and ethnic sections of cities are, quite to the contrary, where the arts are most immediate and full of life. If there are any culturally disadvantaged ghettos, they are probably to be found in white suburbs. . . . For art to reach ethnic audiences, it must relate people to who and what they are— not to what someone else would like them to appreciate or hope they can become. The notion of the arts as something separate and apart from what happens to us every day, as icons to be revered by well rehearsed members of a club on special occasions, has no place and no meaning on the streets of Cleveland's Hough District, the Watts area of Los Angeles, or 119th Street in Harlem. The emphasis in such places is on the content of what is presented and the involve-

76

ment of those who experience it. Technique is, as it should be, a secondary concern for successful . . . ethnic art, which focuses attention on the quality of living. Our established institutions fail to realize that "quality" and "standards" are not in the least at stake. If anything, standards will be expanded, not lowered, as so many argue when seeking to dodge the real issue.

Disadvantaged students are concerned that their teachers do not bother to understand their language or their life style. In particular, the students are extrasensitive to the fact that their teachers never see any good in their culture, habits, and background, or know their heroes and idols. Moreover, their tutors question their slang, stereotype their behavior, and do not read their favorite authors or explore their values. The students routinely expect the teachers to criticize their communication skills. If the students are black, they know that they are automatically expected to accept white standards—standards which many young blacks now reject.

Disadvantaged students reject cultural deprivation theories for other reasons. They know that much of what happens in their culture has a parallel in the dominant culture. They know, for example, that there are no more divorces among their own parents than there are among the parents of the nondisadvantaged. They know that, like their own fathers, fathers in middle-class homes do not normally discuss world problems at the dinner table; and those members of the disadvantaged who have worked as maids, waitresses, waiters, bellhops, motel clerks, and madams can report on the moral, spiritual, and social values of their customers, including teachers.

Students know that their success, or lack of it, is less a factor of their cultural deprivation than it is of good teaching and quality education. They cannot understand how instructors with M.A.s and Ph.D.s who are reputed to be experts in their fields, who claim to like students, and who have been consistently evaluated as effective teachers reach an academic menopause when it comes to producing a sound education for the disadvantaged.

Disadvantaged students observe, are sensitive to, and understand the attitudes of their instructors in other ways too, more so than one might suspect. They constantly point out that their instructors avoid relationships with them, never get to know them as people (Sanford, 1967; Morgan, 1970), and are never aware of their emotional distresses and economic burdens. The students say that their teachers are not concerned about what they think or how they feel. And, they emphasize that no thread of continuity between subject matter and compassion is ever discernible—no warmth, no advice or counsel, no real-life encounter, never a brief pause at the cafeteria table to exchange pleasantries. Faculties rarely extend to, or accept from, the disadvantaged an invitation to exchange away-from-school visits or other positive communication.

Teachers of the disadvantaged never feel as secure to expose their ignorance as they do their knowledge to the students. Students are constantly looking for the things that make their teachers human, but they find that only the negative attitudes of the instructors betray their human qualities.

The least sophisticated among the disadvantaged know that faculty members do not expect much of them academically and never discover what talents they may have. They say that teachers do not anticipate or believe that they have the ability to create and to develop knowledge and are surprised when they do. Instead they accuse disadvantaged students of being disinterested, incapable of learning, and immature. Because of these expectations and accusations, disadvantaged community college registrants believe that their instructors find teaching them less satisfying than they find teaching others. They seem to be running scared, to be up-tight, and to get ulcers on the spot when they must deal with the disadvantaged for any considerable time. These students are aware that their professors are not committed to teaching them. They know that faculty members favor the natural winners in society and not its consistent losers.

Teachers who do not want to teach them and who say so win the respect of the students because they are honest enough to say how they feel. Others are not so honest; but whether the teachers confess or not, the word gets around. In some colleges, faculty members even feel they should have extra compensation for working with the disadvantaged.

The students express many other resentments toward their teachers. They contend, for example, that their instructors work only to serve their own interests. To illustrate, the students point out that teachers assist in making out the class schedule to ensure that it serves their convenience and meets their needs at the expense of the students' needs. Poor students cite the compacted instruction day (usually eight to noon or nine to one) as an example of this self-serving behavior. This situation is of particular significance for the student who must work and attend school after two. One eastern community college president states, "At 2:30 p.m. you can shoot a cannon down the corridor of any building on this campus and never hit anything human unless it is a student or custodian." Disadvantaged students also resent the fact that they are used as the subjects of proposals to obtain grants from the federal government. Once the project is funded, the students know that they profit little from the resources. They have watched government funds stop and programs die because the institution abandoned them. They see the same instructors who refuse or claim inability to teach them apply for and get the job of teaching them to earn extra money. A former New Careers student, now a teacher in a Chicago community college, attacks this hypocrisy with biting rhetoric: "Put some bread in the pen and my colleagues are the first hogs to the trough." At a Title V Institute for Junior College Teachers of the Disadvantaged from Urban Ghettos, the rhetoric was sharp (DeNevi, 1970):

Most junior college teachers in the ghetto live neatly compartmentalized lives. Man, they actually feel sentenced to teach slum youth. They only put up with it because they need the bread— the bastards. Their teaching is passionless. Their empathy with those they teach, with the surrounding community, is nonexistent. Their jobs, like their lives, are counterfeits: dry lectures substitute for teaching; confrontations with students replace counseling. Ghetto teachers flee back to their tidy suburban pods for what little redemption they

79

get from cocktails or nagging wives. What is needed are seasoned professionals: professionals who are not gelded, who listen and teach with a skill that lends warmth and hope to lives which often hang by slender threads.

Students learn other things about their middle-class teachers. They learn, for example, that while the legislature, trustees, and administration open the doors of the college to disadvantaged students, the faculty close the curricula to them, that they are not partners in the learning process and therefore the instructor dictates all the terms for learning, that their instructors conduct only monologues with them—never dialogues. Most of all they discover that subject matter is sacrosanct. This worship of subject matter does two things: (1) As Morgan (1970) indicates:

Imparting volumes of subject matter without priorities or relevance becomes the goal. The strategy is to avoid relationships with the students in spite of the fact that these relationships are probably necessary for the students to learn. Instead of forming relationships the fearful teacher takes flight into sacredness of subject matter and technique. The student is overlooked as a person who is looking for help.

(2) It also says that the teacher considers himself the most important human component—not the student. Consequently, he tolerates little inquiry from the disadvantaged. He does not encourage or expect these students to raise issues. The students never have an opportunity to experience the subject matter as a dialogue between generations but see their teachers constantly revive the past and fail to connect it to the present. Disadvantaged students believe that their tutors would be lost without their painstakingly compiled notes, and they are convinced that their teachers feel that the only way that education progresses is through the proliferation of books. They do not like the lectures. The lecture is one of the most primitive, most used, and most ineffective teaching methods. Teaching is

dynamic. It requires hard work, changing, adjusting, and relating to and interacting with the learner—not a daily monologue.

Although community college students do not really care about the academic activities of their teachers, they are well aware (as others are) that the scholarship and professionalism that their teachers boast about is a fraud since community college teachers as a whole do virtually no original study and since their tenure, promotions, and salaries do not depend upon their involvement with research and publication. Students are further aware that too many of their teachers demand to take part in decision-making activity and do not spend time in meetings having to do with the combined activities of teaching, learning, advising, academic leadership, and other functions necessary to provide for good supervision of instruction.

These problems are epic in their implications. Yet, little is ever done about the attitude and behavior of teachers toward their students. This problem is a constant concern whenever work with the disadvantaged is being examined. The consistent component in the Kerner report (1968), the Coleman report (1966), and the hundreds of other studies on the disadvantaged is the negative attitude of teachers toward the disadvantaged and the implications of those attitudes for the learning process. The Kerner report said it this way: "Studies have shown that the attitudes of teachers toward their students have very powerful impacts upon educational attainments. The more teachers expect from their students—however disadvantaged those students may be—the better the students perform. Conversely, negative teacher attitudes act as self-fulfilling prophecies: the teachers expect little from their students; the students fulfill the expectations." The Kerner report corroborates the findings of Jacobson and Rosenthal (1967) and Clark (1965).

In spite of the two-year college pronouncements, too many disadvantaged students see the community college as the graveyard of any hope they have for getting an education. "Fortunately," as one youngster puts it, "God don't grade on the curve." In spite of the harshness of their rhetoric however, one would be remiss if he did not emphasize that disadvantaged students are the first to recognize the qualities of what they consider good teachers and administrators. Teachers who attempt to understand them, require them to work hard, care about their problems, listen to their points of view, disagree with them when they are wrong, praise them when they deserve it, and say in their presence what they say in their absence are prized by disadvantaged students—or any student, for that matter. These teachers' classes are the first to fill, and the students know that they need not hesitate to approach them when they have a problem, academic or otherwise. Students do not hesitate to compliment administrators who exhibit these qualities. Most of all, they appreciate the administrator who is fair, consistent, and aware of what is going on in his institution. They pass the word along to the other students. It is common to hear these students say, "I know where he is coming from" or "I know where his head is."

What many do not realize is that disadvantaged students are more aware of their shortcomings than are those people who constantly allude to their deficiencies. These students are the ones who have received the poor grades, are the subjects of negative reports on anecdotal records, have been ignored and treated unfairly by administrators, have been turned down in employment offices, and receive welfare checks. They do not need tutors to tell them this. And if they are minority group people, they do not need the sensitivity games played by some counselors and teachers. They leave participation to middle-class youngsters who feel the need to have someone tell them how he really feels about them. Minority group students already know. The whole life of most disadvantaged students has been a continuous sensitivity session. Each day carries with it a new encounter. They do not need their teachers to make them aware of what they are. They want teachers and administrators who can make them aware of what they can be. In a word, they want their teachers to be human; and they praise them when they are.

What can be done to improve learning in educationally disadvantaged students? The realistic administrator is well aware that open doors for the disadvantaged require commitment from all quarters of the college community, and he knows that this commitment has never been made. It is even less available now than previously because existing minimal open admissions and accessibility to higher education for the disadvantaged are under serious threat from all parts of the academic community, and there has been a corresponding curtailment in government and foundation funds to assist in providing a quality education for the disadvantaged. Few colleges invested their own financial resources in an attempt to improve education for this group except as matching funds required for certain federal and foundation grants. This lack of institutional investment is evidence of the low commitment of the faculty and administration—a commitment which has been challenged because some of the disadvantaged have taken part in student activism. All parts of the academic world and people of influence outside are still engaged in the great debate: Should disadvantaged students be admitted into the college in the first place? Resistance comes from all sides.

Many faculty feel, as we have seen, that the cumulative effects of cultural deprivation are irreversible by the time the student is in college. They say that they can neither teach nor reach the disadvantaged. And their performance at present makes it abundantly clear that this is an accurate statement. College registrars would reject the admission of the disadvantaged because these students do not follow procedures, do not get information in on time, and require special staff and handling. Furthermore, they contend that to admit these students into the college excludes many other students who are better "qualified." Registrars maintain that such admissions constitute discrimination in reverse. College business managers, hard-headed, practical men, say that it takes much more of everything to educate disadvantaged students than it does to educate normal (whatever that means) students. This means that it costs more. A number of psychologists have suggested that it is unkind to take these students into the college and raise their hopes only to see them fail and become frustrated. Faculty senates resent the implication of having to lower admissions standards. Admissions officers say that the dropout rate is higher; librarians say that these students cannot make the best use of printed resources; even the vice-president of the United States is opposed to providing special admissions consideration to disadvantaged students. I have just mentioned a few of the people who claim that admitting the disadvantaged into the college is nothing more than a benevolent experiment that is doomed to failure. Each person has his own personal reason. If he does not he makes one up.

Most of these individuals reach their decisions without the benefit of first-hand knowledge or even reading about the people who they say should be excluded. Their reasons or excuses, depending upon one's point of view, deserve examination. Those who say that the cumulative effects of race, class, and economic situation have been so devastating that learning is highly improbable and the situation is irreversible must be totally unaware of the thousands of students who go to college each year with those exact handicaps and successfully complete their education with and without special assistance. And other students who do not have such handicaps nonetheless are unsuccessful in school.

Registrars who claim that the disadvantaged require extra work are right. But their offices exist to provide a service to the institution and to the student. And they cannot possibly be as unsophisticated and insensitive to the institutional facts of life as their statement of reverse discrimination indicates. The education system has always been discriminatory—philosophically and practically. A good halfback who was poor, academically slow, and racially different always got preferential treatment at the expense of "qualified" students, as did the sons of important alumni and donors of fiscal and physical resources and the students too poor to pay tuition, too slow to do college work, but capable of playing a great tuba in the marching band. I asked a registrar about this discriminatory admission and his reply was, "That's different, each one of those is a special person!" Everyone is. The registrar's statement indicates precisely why the administrator needs to be keenly aware of how those around him feel about open doors for the disadvantaged.

For teachers to say that they can neither teach nor reach the disadvantaged is inexcusable. Both of these skills can be learned. The first requires learning the techniques of the profession. The second requires knowledge of the world of the disadvantaged and personal involvement with the students. If left completely to their own choices, most community college people would find it easier to work toward making their institutions junior and four-year colleges than to learn to teach the disadvantaged.

The business officer is right. It does take more money to educate a student who is disadvantaged than one who is not. But it is equally true that it requires more money to keep a man in prison than to send him to college; it costs more to field a football team than to develop a good reading program; it costs more to pay a professor than a teaching assistant, although the latter does all the work even though the student pays his tuition and has a right to get the professor. Somehow, it seems more important to monitor cost factors with regard to the disadvantaged than with regard to other groups.

The psychologist who says we should deny disadvantaged admission to the college because it is unkind to raise hopes in view of the probability of failure is unaware or disregards the research in his own discipline and the student's need for hope, right of access to the college (both by statute and philosophy), and right to equality of opportunity. If these reasons are too philosophical, consider the fact that the student or his parents or both pay the psychologist's salary. And, as we have noted, considerable evidence reveals that the prediction and expectation that students will fail is a self-fulfilling prophecy (Jacobson and Rosenthal, 1967).

The admissions officer is wrong about the dropout rate. Reynolds (1969 and 1970) and Pollard (1970) found that the attrition among the disadvantaged students was no higher than that among college students as a whole. There is rarely a 50 per cent dropout rate among the disadvantaged in the special programs which have been designed for them.

As for the faculty senate, it is not a student-centered organization in the first place. Still it operates in an institution which has as its basic philosophy the concept of providing quality education to a broad population—a college- or university-bound group (usually the only one the senate is concerned about), a vocationally oriented group, and a continuing education group. The program for each group has separate standards, some of them established outside the college. A faculty senate by the very fact that it exists within an institution with this philosophy should accept that philosophy and is in no position to refuse to admit the disadvantaged on the grounds that standards must be lowered.

Finally, the librarian would be the first to admit that a community college is lucky to have a 25 per cent book circulation with its advantaged students, assuming he can tell who is and who is not advantaged. He also knows that book circulation, or lack of it, is not clear evidence as to what students are learning or not learning. Moreover, books are only one of the items which should be available in the instructional resource center. Recordings, films, prints, sculptured models, and so forth are also learning resources—ones that are more effective than books for the disadvantaged. In fact, the whole idea of American Library Association standards being indicative of the quality of the education in a community college needs further examination.

As to the vice-president of the United States, Dennis W. Binning, editor of *College and University Business,* commented on a speech that Spiro Agnew made opposing open admissions. Agnew said, "When I need a doctor, I don't want one who was admitted to medical school on a quota system." Binning's response (1970): "The proposition seems unassailable until one considers that *the thing to worry about is not how the doctor was admitted but how he was graduated.*" Carl Rowan, a Washington columnist with the typical candor of a black, was more blunt (1970):

Only a calculated maliciousness could provoke the number two elected official to try to convince a troubled, ill-informed populace that the woes of society arise from a "new socialism" that sets up college "quotas" for minority groups. An enlightened official ought to be explaining that our troubles run deep precisely because for too long the colleges had quotas that kept all but a few minority group members out.

All the persons opposed to the admission of disadvantaged

students agree that they should have an opportunity for additional education. There is also a consensus that these students should have some remedial reading, mathematics, and English. All agree that this is what is needed to solve the education problem. Hence, we have a group of people who, by their own admission, know virtually nothing about the disadvantaged but who are opposed to their admission into the college. At the same time, these people have agreed upon a prescription to solve the educational problem of the group—remedial work. Education made simple.

Most people who resist admission of the disadvantaged into the college are more concerned about what the student is (test scores, reading level, grade point average) when he is admitted to college than about what he is when he leaves. In short, they are more concerned with the raw material than with the eventual product. These critics are more concerned with selecting the students to be admitted than with getting them through a well defined and well developed program once they are admitted.

The administrator should know some of the other reasons why faculties are not committed to education of the disadvantaged since they offer so much resistance to it. Students watch a few dedicated college people in special programs begging other faculty members to take an active role in providing for the disadvantaged. And they see 98 per cent of those asked turn down the opportunity. Consequently, programs for these groups are usually staffed by people new to the college who do not know the structure, politics, or techniques for negotiating the system.

One reason for their reluctance to staff these programs, they claim, is that their colleagues charge them with watering down their subject matter in order to teach the disadvantaged. They are also accused of teaching to the gallery when they present subject matter efficiently and in a form that is clear to the student. These teachers are more concerned about the appraisal of their colleagues than they are about providing good instruction to students who need it. This professional ridicule from their peers pressures them into running with the herd. Elementary school teachers are taught that when a student fails to grasp their material, they must try another technique;

they must teach in the student's learning style and at his pace and conceptual level. It is more important that the student learns than that the subject matter be preserved in a form the learner cannot deal with quickly and effectively. A professor who refuses to make adjustments in what he teaches so that the learner can understand it makes the material more important than the function it is supposed to serve.

Another problem which I alluded to before is that college parallel faculties would prefer that the community colleges become miniuniversities and reflect the poor man's privileged elite replete with stringent selection requirements, faculty rank, a specified number of Ph.D.s on the staff, and a considerable amount of other nonsense which would be totally inappropriate for the two-year college and its teaching function (Medsker, 1960; Roueche, 1968). Therefore, high-risk students count on very minimal assistance and commitment from college parallel faculty. In this group of academicians, the disadvantaged can see only the arrogance and pageantry of scholarship, which has stripped them of their compassion for the student. They know that the doors to the college transfer program are not really open to them. The doors are barely ajar.

In many areas of the vocational and technical divisions of the community college, one finds this same lack of commitment to the disadvantaged student. To be sure, many of them are enrolled in the vocational programs. But, except in certain programs which require minimal skills, vocational people too want their students to be bright (and white) and also do everything they can to ensure that they are.

It is an old saying that a student who cannot work with his mind can work with his hands, even though one must caution the man who is about to take his automobile to a mechanic who works only with his hands. This whole idea of choosing a trade if one cannot do academic work, however, implies that the academically disadvantaged would be better seeking vocational instruction rather than academic instruction. But vocational people resent this implication. They do not want disadvantaged students in their classes—further evidence of their lack of commitment to these students. And since many of them are card-carrying hard hats, they do not encourage entry of nonwhite disadvantaged students in their programs at all.

In spite of the attitude of college parallel people toward their subject matter, they at least let a student in who they think is qualified and can make it. Once in, the student must shoot for himself. The vocational people, on the other hand, try hard to keep out the disadvantaged and minority group student. If he gets in, however, instructors in vocational areas spend much time helping him.

The vocational staff suffers from another problem. They frequently are treated as second-class citizens—as though they are less than professional—by the college parallel staff. Not infrequently, the administration aids and abets this academic snobbery. Local and national professional organizations also support some of this snobbery by not admitting into their ranks instructors who do not have academic degrees. This is another reason why vocational people want to keep out students who they think will lower the quality of the program.

It is interesting to compare the commitment and assistance of college parallel and vocational people to the disadvantaged and contrast the behavior of these two groups with that of the community service group. The community service faculty are much more committed to disadvantaged students than either of these other groups is, although they do not receive enough support from the rest of the college. They do not worship subject matter or worry about union influence. They offer basic education to middle-age dropouts and illiterates, college exploratory courses to war veterans, and teacher-aide programs to New Careers enrollees. I have explained their role elsewhere (Moore, 1970a):

This faculty, perhaps more than either of the other two, exemplifies what the community college is all about. It makes the abstract platitudes and philosophy about the "open-door" character of the community college a concrete reality. The members of this staff work with an entire community—go where they are invited, get involved, and make education relate to what the people in the

*community say their needs are. They do not prescribe a course,
curriculum, or program, and say to a community, "These are your
needs." This faculty does not set up criteria to select certain students
and exclude others. And one never finds the punitive items in the
community service catalog or brochure that he finds in the transfer
and vocational sections of the college handbook or catalog, namely
all the ways he can fail (lack of attendance, withdrawal penalties,
rules of conduct, dress, and so on).*

Faculty, however, can be found guilty of other undesirable practices.
In many prevocational, preapprentice, and precollege programs the
students never get beyond the prefix. Millions of dollars have gone
into programs to teach low-level skills that were obsolete the day
the students enrolled. Such practices only make the student aware
that he is at a dead end. Thousands of students have gone through
several different programs and have not been able to secure jobs
requiring the skills they were taught. Community college people
have written many of the proposals for and have established these
programs. They have recruited temporary people, have borrowed
space temporarily from other divisions, and have worked with students who did not realize that they too were temporary.

Just as lack of commitment to the disadvantaged is reflected
in the various programs of the college, it is also evident in the curriculum design and offerings. Curriculum for the disadvantaged has
not changed in fifty years. It is still the same remedial triad. We
still attempt to teach people to write and speak by teaching them
grammar, to read by lowering the grade level of the material and
by making the plots less sophisticated, and to do mathematical
reasoning and computation by assigning page after page of drill
material that is totally unrelated to what the student does in real
situations. In the first case, it is well established that the best way
to learn to write is to write. One soon learns those few elements of
grammar—and they are few—that he needs to know. Once he has
learned these few elements, he knows as much about grammar as his
teachers know, with the exception of his English teachers. This
latter group of teachers knows all about grammar but rarely writes

anything that a significant part of the populace ever reads. A few of them write textbooks.

The Watts writing workshops, conceived by the author and screenwriter Bud Shulberg, have shown that students can do some excellent writing, even though they know virtually nothing about the structure of the language, when they are motivated to concentrate on their ideas and feelings. When students are assigned to write about their experiences, they write with insight, with sharp attention to details, with rich colloquialism, and with stark, raw passion. They also reveal their great humanity and that small pinch of arrogance that adds tension to the personality and thus dynamism. What the disadvantaged student faces in most remedial English classes is workbook exercises to do, blanks to fill in, endings to change, verbs to conjugate, friendly letters to write, and some expository themes to compose. Students reject—and they should—this kind of archaic pabulum. These students frequently have more experiences than do those who teach them. The material that is a part of their life style, a part of their triumphs and adversities, is the subject matter to which disadvantaged students respond and on which they can write.

The mathematics taught to disadvantaged students is equally in need of attention. We ask the student to do excessive numbers of drill exercises in isolation, or if he is above the fractions-decimal-proportions-percentage level of arithmetic, we assign him algebra. Yet few instructors or professors not in mathematics or a related field can work out enough algebraic principles to develop the class schedule, and, in fact, one has difficulty documenting the need for the algebra we get in school for 95 per cent of the population. For the disadvantaged, mathematics should be related to how the landlord, furniture store merchant, loan company official, and others who do business in the ghetto fleece him. Mathematics should also be related to what the student expects to do when he is through school. If he wants to be a photographer or barber or advertising man, algebra probably will not help him. There is value in teaching algebra if it has some relationship to what the student wants to do or is absolutely necessary as a prerequisite to advanced work.

Blind Man on a Freeway

Reading is the third component of the remedial triad normally applied to disadvantaged students when we open the doors of higher education to them. Morgan (1970) notes that "teachers are usually out of touch with their students' real concerns and continue to teach them reading by feeding them materials which picture them as dehumanized and degraded." He further points out that when disadvantaged students, especially black ones, are assigned materials which are pertinent and interesting to them "their reading appetites are wide and ravenous." *Soul on Ice, The Autobiography of Malcolm X, Custer Died for Your Sins, Nobody Likes a Drunken Indian, La Raza,* and so forth are never prescribed for disadvantaged students to read. They are still required to read *Call of the Wild* and a series of other classics or some of the other traditional materials.

Moreover, the student is taught to read by using a series of techniques, one of which is usually a speed test each day. I am told that doctors and lawyers are taught to read slowly, to digest what they read, and to ask many questions of themselves as they read. This does not mean that slow readers are necessarily better readers. The opposite is true. But if a student must read slowly in order to comprehend and digest the material he reads, he should read slowly, commensurate with his comprehension rate and learning style. Paradoxically, we expect and teach our poorest readers to read fastest. And we base a part of their reading evaluation upon speed reading.

Finally, reading is best learned by reading. Vocabulary exercises, phonics, and other such methods used effectively with young children are frequently a waste of time with young adults. Angry, street-educated, disadvantaged college students are not about to strut around in class with their mouths contorted and looking silly to make a series of "ahs" and "oos" in order to read about "an affair of a lilac with a drop of rain."

Good curriculum has quality and substance. It is related to and has application in real life situations. It is planned not only with the society and subject matter in mind but also with the learner in mind. A quality curriculum has flexibility, opportunities for stimulating creativity, the means to help the student cope with his environment, and an opportunity for the student to produce knowledge. In the community college, the curriculum for the disadvantaged must be a knowing and a doing course of study to meet the various needs of the registrants. If the curriculum is not, then the people who planned it were not committed to quality education for the disadvantaged; those who approved it were seeking little more than a stop-gap method to solve one of the most significant educational problems of our times; and if the remedial treadmill is the only method explored to provide instruction to disadvantaged students, then the administration, faculty, and counselors are only espousing the rhetoric of hypocrisy. Disadvantaged students call this "talking that talk."

Thus, except for what they see in the community service area, students are aware that they have only tenuous commitment from the faculty and the administration. They understand that they have support as long as someone else pays the bill. Also, no adjustment has to be made in the normal business and routine of the college as long as the disadvantaged remain on the periphery and as long as they keep their noses clean. This latter criterion means to avoid getting involved in sit-ins, making demands, and engaging in other activist activities which question or challenge the system. In sum, they should not attempt to buck the system. "After all," comments one dean in a Texas community college, "these kids are here to get 'a good education' not to question everything." High-risk students test the commitment of those who claim to be interested in them early in their college experience. It is a common maneuver to involve themselves in disconcerting, if not norm-violating, behavior to watch the reaction of college people. They are deliberately loud as they talk in groups to see whether this will evoke "I told you so" attitudes and statements (and glances) from faculty members. Male students often wear their hats in class or produce a unique strut when they walk. Blacks especially adapt mannerisms which drive many whites up a tree—clenched fists, different vernacular, unique styles of dress, and natural hair styles. This does not mean that a particular student who clenches his fist, uses the prevailing vernacular, wears his hat in the classroom, wears the dress of his peers, and has a natural or afro hair style is a militant. Many of them have natural hair-dos and processed minds. (Processed hair has been straightened and styled to look like that of whites.) Minority group students have special names for these pseudomembers. Orientals call them bananas (yellow on the outside, white on the inside), blacks call them oreos, and Chicanos call them coconuts. Minority group students among the disadvantaged like to know exactly where people stand on issues, and they often measure commitment by observing the reactions of persons to them, particularly those persons who profess loyalty to them.

Disadvantaged students also know that they are "special." The institution does not let them forget it. The college normally registers the students as a group and has their books all "shopping-bagged-up" and tagged so that they do not go through the same lines, make the same errors, negotiate the same red tape, and follow the same process as other students. Often they look like mice following a pied piper (their director or counselor) around the campus during the first few days of orientation. This kind of debasement could be eliminated by bringing the students on a few days early and taking them through a dry run. This too is spoon-feeding, but when the student returns on registration day, he looks like every other student. There is nothing to distinguish him from any other student. These students need not always be subtly informed that somebody is doing something for them.

All these attitudes and actions are related to commitment. The college (and the administration) should do everything to preserve the dignity of the student. It cannot operate on the principle that the students ought to be happy they got in. As I have described here, many special efforts ought to be made to develop effective teaching techniques to work with disadvantaged students. This special attention is what any group of students needs whether they are honor or remedial. The college is often, though not always, willing to commit itself and make the adjustment to meet the needs of the honor students, but the remedial students are asked to adjust. It must be said, however, that whether the group is honors or remedial, the instruction is usually the same. It rarely changes. The professor prescribes the remedy (material to be learned) and the method. If the one he prescribes does not work, he blames it on the patient's condition (cultural deprivation, lack of ability, poor skills). He rarely changes the remedy, and because he treats all the patients with the same one, he frequently ignores learning style and other specific needs and characteristics of students and, therefore, is often providing inappropriate instruction for many of his students. The professor is a great deal like the medicine show doctor of western folklore. His snake oil is advertised to cure disease. But if the patient is too sick (IQ "too low," Board scores not high enough), today's doctor reserves the right not to treat him at all or refuse to treat him because he's too near dead. This is hardly a commitment.

Basically, however, commitment to the educationally disadvantaged on the part of the institution (which, as I have indicated here, is the only avenue to changing their situation) begins and ends with commitment to the concept of the open door and its implications. The administrator cannot confuse open doors for the disadvantaged student with open doors for a student who is simply economically poor.

Colleges have always accepted the poor student who has ability, can earn a scholarship, can negotiate the education establishment, and can work his way through. Such a student can handle the communication skills, does not challenge the system, makes good grades, and does not make waves. He is a fine student in the Horatio Alger tradition. He grows up, becomes a member of the alumni association, and joins the ranks of those who cannot understand why other poor students cannot pick themselves up by their bootstraps. Many thousands of immigrants who struggled through the system and now are a participating part of it characterize this student. Thousands of black and other minority students went through the same education system in the same way and not only have been rejected as human beings but also have been prevented from entering the system. These were students who had ability but were the wrong color or nationality or religion or all three. Disadvantaged students simply do not see this as commitment. No way.

Blind Man on a Freeway

It would serve little purpose here to list and discuss the programs or, as it were, the open door and corresponding commitment for the disadvantaged. Gordon and Wilkerson (1966) surveyed compensatory education in over six hundred colleges with special attention to and comment on the community college. Egerton (1968) did a similar study in 215 colleges and universities. Moore (1968b, 1968c, 1968d, 1970a) describes programs or lack of them for the educationally disadvantaged. In like manner, Roueche (1968) explores the problems and the opportunities for the disadvantaged in the community college, and Knoell (1966, 1968, 1970), too, examines opportunities for this group of students. The Department of Health, Education, and Welfare (1969) describes career opportunities for the disadvantaged and handicapped. There are, in fact, a large number of programs for the disadvantaged all over the nation. While the number of programs has increased, there has not been a commensurate documentation of these efforts to determine their success. Teaching methods, materials used, counseling techniques, means used to sell the program to the rest of the college, strategies used to absorb and make the program an on-going part of the college program, and overall approach used to attack the educational, personal, and social problems of disadvantaged students have not been evaluated. When there is an infrequent evaluation of a program, it is usually done too soon after the program has been initiated and by using the same old methods.

Success in many programs has been evaluated on the basis of attrition rate, one of the poorest indices. The one common denominator among all these alleged dropouts is that they do not take the time to officially withdraw. However, this simplistic classification needs redefinition. Follow-up studies show that students leave projects for many reasons. Some students leave because they are ill, some find good jobs, some are called into the armed services, some get married, some change their goals, others accomplish a new goal of which the college is unaware, still others simply flunk out, and many get fed up and quit.

One program, at certain times of the year, had a great influx of students considered disadvantaged who were interested in math and English skills. After about eight weeks in the program, a significant number of these students dropped out, apparently without good reason since many were doing well in their courses. Investigation revealed that a large number of the students worked at the Post Office, which scheduled periodic Civil Service examinations for workers. If a worker passed the examination, he was eligible to move up to a higher job in the postal service. Consequently, after a student passed the Civil Service test, he stopped attending the English and mathematics classes; he accomplished his goal. Was he a dropout? In terms of rules, the answer has to be affirmative. In terms of the student's goal, the answer is a definite no, indicating that perhaps the classification is not meaningful and that the success of these programs should be evaluated on a basis other than the traditional ones.

As a reader of proposals submitted to funding agencies and as a consultant to more than three hundred community and senior institutions, I can hypothesize why many of these programs do not succeed and the hypotheses have nothing to do with attrition, to put it bluntly. Institutions serve their own interests at the expense of the disadvantaged. Only about one college in one hundred includes in its proposal the intent to make the special program for the disadvantaged an on-going and integrated segment of the institution. And, in their proposals, a large number of the colleges treat ethnic studies as their only program for the disadvantaged. Such programs should be only one of the options for all students, including advantaged and disadvantaged whites, who probably profit most from ethnic studies. But the problem goes back further than the community college itself. In cases where four-year colleges propose to set up training programs for community college personnel, a cursory look at the staff to be used in the proposed project rarely shows a person with community college experience. Rarely does anyone know anything about high-risk students, their learning problems, habits, talents, expectations, or other characteristics—all of which are so well known about the typical college student. To be sure, students with community college experience whom the colleges want to train are more enlightened about the needs, responsibilities, and requirements of two-year college personnel than are the people hired to teach them.

If this chapter has done little else, it should have alerted administrators to how these students feel about the community college and its personnel; it should have sensitized them to the need to allocate resources on an equitable basis for all programs in the institution including programs for the disadvantaged student; it should have made them keenly conscious of their need for additional training to work in the modern community college—especially one located in an urban community. And, finally, it should have made a strong case for commitment to the educationally disadvantaged.

New Training for
New Leaders

There should be a nationwide drive to prepare and develop administrators and faculty for the community colleges. Although this recommendation has been made many times in the past, we have still to evolve a theory of community college administration. Books on and college courses in educational administration emphasize the four main functions of a college (academic affairs—instruction and research programs; business affairs—financial, plant, and personnel management; student personnel services; and development and public relations) rather than the roles, functions, and tasks of those who administer them. Students of administration are expected to learn the tenets of control, to analyze the organizational structure of educational institutions, to simulate how fiscal resources are allocated and how human resources are coordinated, to know the theoretical concepts of leadership, to have a broad knowledge of higher education, to know some legal aspects of administration, to have some knowledge of facilities planning, and to possess some research skill. This summary of administrative training in our colleges and universities characterizes the academic approach. It prepares administrators (primarily principals and superintendents) to carry on the traditional and routine functions of an educational institution. Past practices, formulas, and precedents help people especially qualified in specific areas to carry out the routine responsibilities. They, however, are not the ones that take most of a community college administrator's time, create the greatest stresses for him, and require almost immediate solutions. Most of the problems we have identified and defined in this volume are outside of the everyday common responsibilities of the administrator, and his educational training did not provide him with either the skill to handle them or the practice in solving other such problems which do not have textbook solutions.

One of the reasons current training programs are inappropriate is that they are designed to be used with a student clientele different from that of the community college. The average age of two-year college students is twenty-five. The administrator, therefore, must work on an adult-to-adult basis with them. Another reason is that a community college has an atypical teaching staff—a mixture of people (academic, vocational-technical, community service) who are not normally found working on the same faculty in a higher education institution. Furthermore, they frequently come from different levels in the educational hierarchy. Some have come from teaching in high school, some from teaching in a university, and some from industry. A community college administrator can expect still other differences: high attrition among his staff and students and a faculty that often looks to both the university model of governance and the public school model of faculty negotiations. These differences alone have implications which justify a special kind of training for community college administrators.

Before we get into a training program for prospective community college administrators, it is important to understand why we do not have such a program and the problems and prospects of evolving one. Administrative (and teacher) training programs

100

for the community college have not evolved because of the nature of the two institutions involved (the university and the community college), the respective attitudes of the people who work in them, the role and function of each institution, the students and other publics they serve, the failure of the community college to articulate its needs to the university, and the lack of desire or the inability of the senior institution to modify old programs and to develop new ones. I shall discuss these situations in some detail.

The community college is the fastest growing segment of higher education (Carnegie Commission on Higher Education, 1970). Universities are aware of this growth and are superficially involved in it. Here and there they have added one or two courses to the curriculum for in-service community college teachers and administrators seeking certification and working on advanced degrees. The majority are simply talk-chalk courses by which the university makes money without providing expertise to people who need purposeful training. The training is done in a hothouse fashion, outside of the real world of the community college; and the involvement shows no real university investment. As a consequence, many two-year college administrators are suspicious of such training and involvement. They are convinced that university participation will not be a cooperative venture.

They generally believe that university people will get involved but on their own terms, that they will take the community college and do to it what they have done to the senior institution. They will resort to the well rehearsed and well known academic rhetoric about "maintaining standards," "qualified staff," and "college level," and to research-based monologues which usually represent the university position. Junior college advocates know this position as one of academic snobbery, one that seldom changes. It is not a mutually facilitating, but a dictatorial, posture. It has been elitist and rigid, an antiposture: antidisadvantaged, anti-high risk; anti-open admissions, antiminority, and antipoor. University people hold the community college in contempt. They have been "skeptical of or hostile to the junior college" (Mallan, 1968), and they treat community college people as though they know what is best for them and the institution they represent. For these reasons, many two-year college people want to put the university on notice that while the community college leadership prefers to be a cooperative partner with the university and needs its expertise in the higher education venture, they will not agree to serve the ends of this institution rather than those of the community from whence they get their support.

Since the nature and function of the university are antithetical to those of the community college, the purported involvement of the university in preparing two-year college personnel seems questionable, unreliable, and invalid. A cursory comparison of the two institutions illustrates their basic differences. The university is an elitist institution which carefully selects its students; it has a history of excluding the poor and certain minorities of color, using a quota system for other minorities, and rejecting students who do not have a history of good academic performance. The community college is an open-door institution, which accepts all students who apply. The university emphasizes research and publication; the community college stresses teaching. Much of the instruction in four-year colleges is done by amateurs (graduate teaching assistants); most of the instruction in the junior college is done by professionals, either degreed professionals or vocational specialists who got their training through apprenticeship programs. The focus of the university is turned inward to the discovery of knowledge and the perpetuation of the institution, while the community college has as its primary focus applying knowledge to the problems and needs of the community it serves. The reward system of the university is tied to credentials; in the community college, rewards are tied to task. Pearl's (1970) statement about this credentialing is directly related to the way community college people (and disadvantaged students) feel about university influence on the junior college.

Because we are a credential society, because we portion out wealth, prestige, and status disproportionately to those who successfully complete a formal education, the university has become the primary vehicle for the maintenance of racism. The precious few numbers of poor minority youth who obtain degrees camouflage the university's apparent true function, which is to help maintain the current inequitable distribution of power and wealth. The continued existence of poverty, the developing of "behavioral sinks" in the inner cities where overcrowding and dilapidation contribute to the degeneration of human relationships, the muddling of our attempts to build model cities—all reflect the failure of the university and its self-proclaimed scholars to come to grips with major social problems. . . . The university is primarily in the business of vocational training. It turns and tailors the student to meet the specifications of the business, medical, legal, educational, and engineering industries. The procedures used reinforce all prevailing prejudices and deny opportunity to the poor and the nonwhite. But the reinforcement of racism is, perhaps, not the university's primary evil; it is conceivable that even more devastating is the low level of competence that results from the process. In the end, the credentialed professional is either palpably unable to perform (trained incapacity, as in the case of the teacher in the ghetto), or he has deceived himself and others that he possesses the requisite skills (delusional competence, as in the case of the teacher in the suburbs).

In the senior institution, only the faculty designs and develops curricula; in the two-year college, citizens from the community are advisory in establishing curriculum—sometimes completely prescribing it. The student body in the university is, or tends to be, homogeneous; in the junior college, the students represent a broad heterogeneity. Universities boast of their tradition; the community colleges boast of their flexibility. It appears, therefore, that these two institutions have contradictory goals.

These contradictions in goals make community college administrators suspicious of the idea that the university will be able to train community college personnel. Kiernan (1967) says it directly: "We should not count on the four-year colleges and universities to train [personnel] for two-year colleges, especially when experiences show that the universities tend to do this in isolation from the realities of two-year college needs and circumstances." The teachers'

103

colleges and universities do not presently turn out effective personnel in higher education. No evidence indicates that this situation is changing or that the university will do for the community college teaching and administrative staffs—both potential and in-service— what it has not done for its own. Community college people point to such things as the accreditation teams composed entirely of people from four-year colleges who evaluate their institutions as a good indication of university insensitivity to two-year college needs. In one case, a senior college member of a western community college accreditation team said that the college would be better if there were more Ph.D.s on the staff. Senior college library standards applied to the community college are another case in point.

The community college copes directly and immediately with the problems caused by a great heterogeneity of educational backgrounds—backgrounds which interact and are coincidental with a diversity of ethnic and racial origins and socioeconomic statuses. Community college personnel do not believe that the university, using the techniques, curricula, and staff that it currently uses, will be able to teach teachers who must instruct students representing the full range of educational preparation from severe deficit, as in the disadvantaged and the high-risk student, to superior achievement. And they will not be able to train administrators to administer institutions with such varied student bodies. They simply cannot develop the positive attitudes in their graduates necessary to meet the needs of community college students.

A large number of community junior college students and teachers say that the university is insensitive to the needs of the disadvantaged, who point out that these administrators and teachers are the way they are because of what they learned or failed to learn in the university. Many blacks, Puerto Ricans, and other minorities have been the victims of and therefore the witnesses to the university function of preserving the status quo.

Two-year college professionals are suspicious of the intent of the university, and the students have already had their suspicions confirmed and documented. At Seattle Central Community College, a group of teachers, administrators, students, community organizers, and others took part in a taped forum, The University as Pimp, which demonstrates that hostility.

You know, the more I watch the behavior of the university, the more I am convinced that it is nothing but a monolithic pimp on the rest of education. . . . Think about it. The U has benefited from every single education act on the books for the last ten years. From Headstart to Upward Bound, from the Teacher Corps to High Education Facilities Act, the U has had its fingers in every project. It gets the money and somebody else does the work. I say it again, the U is the biggest pimp in town. . . . Now it [the university] is wooing the junior college—a fertile new academic broad that is hot and bothered and without love, so to speak. The junior college won't even be a good fight for the old vet. Watch what is happening to community colleges all over the country. The U applies for a grant. It not only convinces the junior college folks to endorse it, but also it convinces them to use their own people as guinea pigs, their own space for internships, and to actually train the students. If the project is a success, the U gets the credit and another grant. If the show is a failure, the junior college is responsible. After all, the program and the students were really under the auspices of the J.C.

Yet, it is of little value to expend excessive energy damning the university. Maggie Taylor, a former New Careers student who is currently a teacher in a Chicago community college, says it succinctly: "There isn't much use of spending a lot of time in arguing about which one is worse [the community college or the university]; when it comes to poor folks, they are both hogs at the same trough. The university has just been there longer. We have been telling Charley like it is now for ten years. So far as I'm concerned, it's time to do something. Those junior college leaders need to start doing something."

The community college has the option of training and developing its own experts. There are already enough competent people in its ranks to devise such training. Some junior colleges (Seattle

Central Community College, for example) provide in-service training to their own staffs and award credit which can be applied to move on the salary schedule. The great teacher institutes held in 1970 at Westbrook College in Maine are another case in point. It makes a great deal of sense for the community colleges to seek more grants than they are now awarded. Junior college personnel represent every conceivable discipline; many have graduated from the same universities which claim to prepare teachers. It is sometimes forgotten that the largest number of people at work in the community college are those who have left the senior institutions, and many of them have well developed research skills. The community college must explore this option. It has many exciting possibilities.

If a viable training program for community college administrators is to be evolved, community college people have to be explicit in articulating the open-door philosophy and its implications to the university. It is necessary for them to clearly indicate to the four-year people what the specific needs of the open-door colleges are, both for the disadvantaged and the nondisadvantaged.

The community college must suggest what skills and objectives should be reflected in the curriculum, what books need to be written, what materials should be developed, what specific research needs to be done, what evaluative indices of abilities in community college students should be sought, and what kind of skills they expect in their administrators. And the senior institutions must then be convinced that their graduates in teaching, counseling, and administration can work with a heterogeneous student body. If, after a sufficient lapse of time and after a sufficient number of applicants have been tried, the graduates are still unable to perform the tasks they are hired to do, then the institution which graduates them must be told that future graduates will not be welcome.

Just as the community college has to be specific in providing the university with the data and information necessary to do the job demanded, the university has an obligation of equal importance. It must abandon its dictatorial posture and must listen. It is the layman when it comes to dealing with community college personnel and students. The senior institution has to study the two-year college and its students and stop assuming what it is and what they are supposed to be. A change of method is called for. Graduate professors can no longer lecture and assign term papers and the reading of case studies as the primary training method for administrators. The university has to go back and examine some of its own research and behave as though it believes it or declare it worthless. It has to look at a man's job and determine what skills he will need; then it must provide the specific skills necessary. The dean of student personnel services in the community colleges, for example, has many jobs: He is responsible for the registrar, the admissions officer, student placement, student activities, student government, counseling, student loans, and several other areas of service. A degree in guidance and counseling does not and will not give a man the kind of expertise he needs to perform this job. We hire him, however, and wait two to three years for the secretaries, who are working at one-third or perhaps one-fourth his salary, to teach him to do his job. The graduate institution should change this. Graduates who come to the community college must be trained to be practitioners as well as scholars. It is of little value to the typical two-year college student for his teacher to hold an M.S. or a Ph.D. in theoretical mathematics if he cannot successfully teach ratio and proportion. The university must make internships and other administrative training activities specific and directly related, not incidental, to job practice and expectations.

University people have to change the prevailing attitudes within the academic community to accomplish some of these suggestions—at least in the education department. This is asking a great deal from educators. Change, creativity, innovation, and relevancy are not among their most obvious attributes. It is a travesty that colleges and universities have not developed a systematic method or model specifically designed for training administrative personnel for the fastest growing segment of American education. I feel, however, that community college administrators can be trained once higher education becomes committed and concerned enough to invest its resources.

To develop a bona fide administrative training program, we

start with the man and his job. The administrator in the community college, regardless of his level, must determine his own philosophy for the college, its mission, goals, controls, objectives, and processes, although he rubber-stamps most of the on-going policies, philosophy, methods of operation, legal mandates, traditions, and community demands when he accepts the job. Given these constraints how does he do the job? Any administrator struggling in the fish hooks and barbed wire of the community college should clearly understand that this institution is no place for academic custom. Since he is caught in the backwash of fast, sometimes disturbing, social change, he must be keenly conscious that what is happening in the community college is not transitory phenomena but enduring reality; and he cannot be trapped by old ways of thinking and blinded to the events of the times. He must develop the prodigious patience necessary to cope with resistance to change in the academic community. He must learn, as every administrator has, that the theories and myths his graduate professors preached are found wanting in the bitter realities of practice. Fortunately, students have never listened to their professors; unfortunately, they have always imitated them.

On the job, the community college administrator learns many things which help him in doing his job effectively. He learns the value of a good secretary. She is worth more than another dean. In fact, if one has a choice between the two he should choose the secretary. He learns how to refuse the liaison position of vertical filter and not to make decisions which should be handled above or below his position. He insists, for example, that mid-management personnel (division/department chairmen) assume responsibility for the decisions which should be made at their levels, especially the dirty or unpleasant ones which they usually attempt to avoid. He learns to avoid the trivia (dress codes, hair styles, censorship of the student newspaper, and so forth) which require so much of his time and often are not, in the long view, worth the time and stress. He becomes aware of the futility of attempting to avoid issues and becomes convinced that the main goal is not to return the college to tranquility but to manage the conflict so it can be used in a positive way (and, in so doing, he quickly discovers that consensus management is not as effective as the theorizers suggest). He recognizes the new instruments of learning and learns not to support meaningless curricula whether they are traditional (as English 101 and Western Civilization are in some cases) or are considered innovative. Because of the variant student body, he discovers that it is necessary to stress the equal worth of all facets of the college. He sees the value of being accountable and seeing that others are held accountable for what they do.

From this description of the job, it is clear that the student studying to become a community college administrator has little need for the typical graduate programs of higher education. Almost no one still believes graduate school programs should continue to require Ph.D. candidates to pass one or two foreign language examinations, especially since most never gain proficiency in the languages anyway. Yet, many graduate schools still cling to this archaic requirement. In like manner, the extensive courses in statistics required in many institutions provide the administrative trainee with little background in dealing with the people problems presented in this volume.

Some of the typical higher education courses are obviously necessary to make the community college administrator at least academically respectable and literate in his field. General course requirements for administrative candidates should include the psychologies—of learning, motivation, and abnormality. We do not even have a psychology of teaching the adult. It appears that when you are a postadolescent with a problem, it's pathological. Courses in classroom management, collective bargaining, techniques of teaching, human relations, race relations, and history of minority groups are also important. He should know something about learning style and programed instruction.

Specific administrative courses for each administrative job should also be available. For example, the individual who wishes to be a dean of student personnel services should have specific courses on that role in the community college. They may include The Community College: Administration of/Student Personnel Services in/ Administration of Student Personnel Services in/Evaluation of Student Personnel Services Programs in/Curriculum of/Instruction in/ Counseling in/Nontypical Student in/Typical Student in/and the Community/Independent and Individual Studies in/Student Personnel Services in. The rationale for these courses should be well thought out, and they should be directly applicable to what a student does on the job. At present no such curriculum is specifically designed to deal with each administrative role. I am currently developing such curricula.

Some of these course designations can apply to two-year college administrators other than the dean of students. And some course designations or other programs have not been included. For example, Finance in the Community College, which is quite different from the finance of the university or the secondary school.

In addition, when a candidate discovers the region of his job assignment, he should learn as much about the people of that region as he possibly can. As a good example, if a beginning administrator secures a job in New York City, it would be good sense to learn as much as he can about blacks and Puerto Ricans; if his assignment is in New Mexico or Colorado, he should concentrate on Native Americans and Chicanos. In short, an administrator's training and knowledge should fit the job he is asked to perform and, as much as possible, the place where he expects to work.

In addition to the classroom work which the potential administrator is required to complete, it is also desirable that he serve both an internship and a residency in the community college. Although we claim to have community college leadership programs with well designed internships, such as the W. K. Kellogg Junior College Leadership Program, one has but to read descriptions of the programs or talk to some of the alumni to question their effectiveness. The internship often takes place concurrently with the student's course work. This school-work-observation-participation experience gives him an opportunity to look at all facets of the college and to relate them to what he is studying while he is in the classroom. He

110

has a chance to determine which particular function of the school is best suited to his skills, knowledge, and interest, and, therefore, he can decide early the area of community college work to which he is willing to commit himself. He has an opportunity to compare administrative styles, systems of priorities, uses of authority, effective and ineffective administrators, and planning rationales.

This apprenticeship can be a valuable experience; however, it is an incomplete one. At best, it is only a superficial interim experience, in which the student neither spends enough time nor explores all areas or any one area of the institution in sufficient depth to become an effective administrator in the community college. Interns are more spectators than participants. Theirs is normally the shotgun approach necessary to take an overall look at how the areas of the college mesh. Such an internship is like the old directive teaching experience still prevalent in teachers' colleges. The apprentice or intern teacher is told what lesson he is to teach, when, and who will observe and mark him. The apprentice cannot change the lesson, add things which are not in the lesson plan, or show any initiative. Each week or two, the apprentice moves to a new teacher or administrator.

Such training is not too different from that of the intern who attends meetings with various administrators (department/division chairmen, deans, the president, and the board of trustees) in the community college. His duties and assignments are usually prescribed by his graduate professor. The problem is that the student is more concerned with earning a high grade and pleasing his teacher than with learning how to perform as an administrator. One way to alleviate this problem is to have colleges or universities hire (on a part-time or permanent basis) local community college administrators as their professors in the field and to use the community college as a laboratory and extension of the university and graduate school. In this way the community college administrator fulfills two purposes. First, he sees that the student gets an intern experience appropriate for the job he will have to perform. He is on the spot, in the field, working at the job, and immediately accessible to the student. Second, the community college administrator is an authorized university representative charged with supervising requirements for graduate students. He is responsible to the degree-awarding institution as well as to the college district.

It hardly seems necessary to say that the community college should recruit, help subsidize, and hire nonwhite interns and administrative candidates, even when it does not enroll a significant number of minority group students. Developing an ethnic mix on the staff says to the students, faculty, and community that the doors of the open-door college are as open to professional staff and administration as they are to the students, whereas now there is some question as to whether the doors are open to either.

A well developed residency should be instituted in graduate programs so that the student can spend time assigned to at least two types of community colleges. One should be an inner-city or urban campus which has a mixture of racial and socioeconomic groups, with all the inherent problems and opportunities I have already discussed. The second campus should be a suburban one serving middle-class students. In his residency experience, the student should be expected to zero in on administrative functions which are narrow in scope. If he wishes to gain expertise in student personnel, for example, he should spend his residency working exclusively in that area. He should be expected to work the problems, not watch someone else solve them. That is, he should become the major decision maker for his area of interest. One of the best ways to ensure that he does is to place him in a college which has an administrative vacancy. There are always a number of those around, and he will be as prepared as any other candidate without experience. An arrangement can sometimes be made with an institution to pay one-half of what would normally be budgeted for the position. The school can profit in several ways. It has a full-time administrator at one-half the cost for at least one year. It has the opportunity to train an administrator in the exact manner it chooses to see him grow. It has the option of hiring the candidate when he is awarded his degree (or even before since a Ph.D. degree is not an absolute prerequisite for working in a community college). The college thus gains an administrator who knows before he joins the staff what the community college is all about and the specific skills he must have. All of this is a considerable gain on one-half a salary. To be sure, most of us are only worth one-half of a salary on a new or different job. And even then some of us are overpaid.

An administrative residency is on-the-job training experience under the supervision and guidance of one or more practicing administrators. It requires the trainee to take an active part in the learning-doing process. He learns the jargon of the job to complement the educational jargon he mastered in graduate seminars. He writes educational plans for the next semester, not papers documented with the works of educators whose opinions correspond to his. He is dealing with an actual organizational structure rather than with a theoretical one. The resident has a first-hand opportunity to explore the problems and opportunities of innovation. He watches and participates in the development of budgets, programs, and courses; in faculty and administration selections; in facilities planning; and in union negotiations. He makes decisions which affect the lives of students, faculty, and others. He learns to identify power groups (political, union, professional) on a campus and those who struggle for power. He discovers the adversarial relationship which frequently exists between faculty and administration. He has an opportunity to plan and to participate in planning strategies to secure funds for the college. He has many opportunities to go out and speak in the community and to tell what his college is all about. Most important, he learns to become a specialist at his job.

One cannot say exactly what should be included in the future training of every single student of administration. In the past, educators thought they could. We now know that yesterday's panacea is today's dilemma. One can observe, however, and with increasing agreement among community college administrators and graduate students who have had some opportunity to actively work in a two-year college, that on-the-job training is one of the most effective ways to train an administrator.

Other training models may be tried in the community college

which have not been tried before with administrators. The methods can be used with, or in addition to, a university training program. The visiting lecturer or professor, for example, is a well known and often used teaching resource in higher education. Most often he is an outstanding person in his field, and his name brings prestige to the institution and provides faculty and students with an opportunity to deal with a major authority. I would propose that the same method be used as a training technique for administrators. An outstanding community college administrator such as Joseph P. Cosand of the St. Louis Junior College District could come to a college for one or two years to fill a presidential vacancy. The other administrators working in that college as well as students of administration in nearby colleges and universities could profit from his presence. During this time he could also be grooming or helping to select his successor. If a permanent successor was not desired, available, or located and recruited, another visiting administrator could be sought. The board of trustees of one community college is exploring this proposal. There are definite advantages in changing administrators periodically. For one, administrators who are innovative are usually available; they do not remain long in their posts because most institutions are traditional, and innovation means rocking the boat. Also, new people bring new ideas. And if their tenure is short, they do not build empires, do not bring in their friends, and may not hesitate to make difficult decisions that they might otherwise not make.

Another way a community college may expose the administrative staff to innovation is through an exchange program. Each administrator in the participating group would choose to work at a school different in size, location, enrollment, racial composition, governance, philosophy, financing pattern, and so forth. The receiving institution would have the chance to try a new approach for a period of time, and the administrator would have a new experience.

The District VI community colleges in the state of Washington are administered by an executive committee made up of the chief administrator from each of the colleges in the district. This particular configuration has many advantages. The expertise of all the administrators is brought to bear on a problem. Each administrator knows the rationale for the disbursement of fiscal resources. Politics and preferential treatment of a particular college are eliminated. But, most pertinent here, younger administrators have an opportunity to learn from more experienced ones.

There is also the concept of administering by a task force made up of successful administrators chosen because of their specific skills. This group could go into a college with task-oriented assignments and remain until the problems are solved. They could also teach the other administrators in the institution to solve problems so that they could take over when the experts left.

There are obvious disadvantages in all of these suggestions; but they are all preferable, in my view, to the training in isolation that most of our current administrators have received. With the possible exception of the Kellogg Program, this training has not been in the area of the community college. At least all these methods are practical and make use of the established skills of men on the job. From them each institution can evolve its own model for a training program.

New Recommendations
for New Problems

FIVE

Loss of authority is a common, although unjustified, complaint of administrators. One does not lose authority. It is either taken from him because he is neither strong enough nor competent enough to keep it or he gives it up by his own inaction. He creates a vacuum which someone or some group is willing to fill. Sometimes an administrator loses authority by his failure to fight for his position with his board of trustees, the public, and even the legislature if necessary. Lawmakers have legislated away much of the authority, role, and function of college administrators, but much of the success of this legislation is due to the inactivity of the administrators themselves. Administrators did not speak out, make demands of their own, withdraw their services, raise hell, or organize and approach their legislators (who are supposed to represent them also) and ask them to examine closely what they are doing. One does not see administrators go to the media and explain the side of the administration in

116

the way other groups present their views. Few administrators appear at legislative hearings to voice their concerns because they fear becoming unpopular with faculties. One must inevitably come to the conclusion that many a college president would rather be the president without the authority to carry out the responsibilities of the office than not to be president (or dean or division chairman and so forth). If the present trend is any indication, it is just a matter of time before persons other than the board of trustees will hire an administrator and fire him when he no longer makes popular decisions, regardless of how educationally unsound these popular decisions are or how they affect the students who come for an education or the public who pays the bill.

However, it is not only legislators who have eroded the power of administrators. Today it is common to find faculty and nonacademic staff members asking, demanding, and negotiating to make policy that trustees and presidents should make; making the decisions that deans and department chairmen should make; and resisting change and accountability at the level where they are expected to perform. Only a fool would agree to be responsible for an institution when he is excluded from the decision-making process. But this is precisely what is happening in many community colleges; and the fools are readily available.

Administrators are the academic cowards of our times. They cringe with every threat, get up-tight with every demand, worry about every uncomplimentary line in the daily newspaper, capitulate at the smallest stress, and hide when there is a crisis. Only a few of them appear to have the integrity to stand up and say "no" when it needs to be said or "hell no" when pushed too far. It takes a strong man to subject himself to much of the haranguing that a college leader must expect. But, in the words of an old blues song, "a man ain't supposed to cry." Harry S Truman was more direct. He said, "If you can't stand the heat, get out of the kitchen."

But because they refuse to defend themselves, it appears that administrators believe the characteristics which are too often attributed to them—namely, that they are overpaid, they do little beyond attend meetings, they are inaccessible, they are dishonest, the institution could function equally effectively without them, and the like. When they are attacked, primarily by faculty and legislators, they never counterattack, even though they have all the necessary information and knowledge to do exactly that—and win.

Administrative services are important and needed in the college. If the registrar fails to do his job, the division chairman his, the person who prepares the schedules his, the business officer his, those who say that administrators do nothing find that they cannot carry on an educational program. The people who plan budget models, plan for the construction of new facilities, work in the payroll department to get the checks out on time, or keep up with seniority, sick leave, and earned credits for advancement on the salary scale are all under the cognizance of administrators. Administrators also represent the college to the public, keep the college out of illegal activities, and influence the public and lawmakers who appropriate money. But administrators allow their critics to say they should be doing more. They never bother to say that they, too, have wives and babies to be loved and who want to see them come home to dinner on time some evenings. They never seem to tell their critics that their contact hours number as many as it takes to do the job, including time on nights, Saturdays, Sundays, and holidays. Administrators are without tenure; they do not get preparation time. And their decisions too have helped to bring higher education to its present pinnacle. They have little for which to apologize.

Since most trustees, members of the public, and legislators do not understand what the roles of administrators are, what the levels of their authority are, and what their responsibilities and functions are, one of the primary jobs of the chief administrator should be to tell them. If the chief officer and his staff have refused or have overlooked this important and necessary task, then they do not deserve the titles or the responsibilities of administrators.

Loss of authority is but one of the problems of concern to the administrator, of which none are more significant than the problem of bigotry. Bigotry cannot go on in an instructor's classroom without the knowledge of the department or division chairman or in the college without the knowledge of the directors, coordinators, deans, and president. When such knowledge is widespread and no corrective action is taken, we have in effect a tolerance policy on the part of the administrators. A considerable number of administrators attempt to manage the bigotry charges which reach their attention by placating and isolating the victim so that he will not create too much of a problem. They may convince the guilty instructor or administrator that he should apologize to the student. At other times, they produce the student's academic or behavioral record to subtly intimidate him rather than the perpetrator, thereby failing to take positive and necessary action to get at the problem. This sanctioning method returns the same teacher or administrator to the classroom or his office to repeat the same offense again. And the administrator loses credibility with both the victim and the villain.

Resolving each little charge of bigotry does little to improve the overall situation. If nothing more is done, the climate in the institution gets worse. Separate victims may give up their grievances temporarily, but the cumulative nature of such incidents invariably erupts into open confrontation. Charges and countercharges are made; the newspapers, members of the community, students, and faculty become involved; and the polarity which is a symptom of the divisiveness in our society hardens and becomes entrenched in the community college. It is only a matter of time before the administrator finds that his college is full of hostility, the morale of his staff is low, and he is under constant attack. The problem of bigotry in an institution probably cannot be completely eliminated. It can be alleviated.

An administrator can begin to fight bigotry on the campus by admitting that it is there. It is. To eliminate it, it is best to start with his own team before he attempts to work with the faculty and other staff. There are no specific answers and no cure-alls to the problem. Yet, some methods used previously can be of value. A confrontation workshop with all the members of the administrative staff invited is one configuration which may be used. Minority group leaders from the various organizations discussed in Chapter Two and other minority students from the institution are invited to act as resource people during the first one or two days of the workshop. During the initial series of meetings, these consultants lay it on the line with much hot rhetoric. After this assault subsides—and it will —the administrators have an opportunity to ask for assistance and to ask pertinent questions. They should not hesitate to say to the consultants that the latter have constantly charged the former with saying and doing the wrong things. Now the consultants have the opportunity to indicate what the right behaviors and statements are. Administrators can ask the consultants, for example, what loaded words and phrases they and other members of the staff should avoid. What innuendos should administrators and others be alerted not to make? To what comments about racial and ethnic characteristics do minority group students respond with extreme sensitivity? The administrators can find out what values, rituals, and other culturally related attitudes and activities should not be violated. They can discover what literature to read, what places to visit, and what vernaculars to learn to understand in order to deal with their nonwhite students.

This workshop can also be used as a forum to understand the administrator's role. It should be pointed out to the consultants that administrators and instructors are human. They make mistakes, get angry, respond in irresponsible ways, and slip into stereotyped ways of thinking (some of them in fact do not know any other way of thinking about nonwhites). Some of their behaviors and statements create animosity among nonwhite students and others. The resource people must be made to understand however that each and every incident will not result in a staff member's dismissal from his job; each case will be judged on its own merits. But the administration will take some action. The case will be investigated. The outcome may not always result in dismissal of the person charged, but a report will be made and will become a part of the permanent personnel file with all parties concerned having copies. Since the administrator made the rules and regulations of the institution available to the group during his earlier visits to their headquarters (Chapter Two), the consultants already know what the procedures for dismissal are and what actions are necessary to initiate such a procedure, regardless of the number of demonstrations which are threatened or conducted. If the charges are found to be accurate but are insufficient to require dismissal, the guilty person will neither be assigned to nor remain in a position where further damage can be done. If this means transferring the person, it will be done. If the individual chooses to resign, it will be encouraged. If the individual wants to do something to improve his attitudes and actions, he will be helped.

The consultants may also be asked to help the administrators in thinking through the ramifications of policies which can be discriminatory. They can be asked to identify what existing policies, rules, and procedures should be reexamined and, if possible, eliminated. At the same time, the consultants should be asked to supply alternatives, if not at the time of the workshop, then later as a part of committee work on the problems.

After the rhetoric of the students, the conferees are ready for some objective evidence. In small groups (two or three) the administrators should accompany the consultants to the areas of the city where the consultants live. The administrators can experience the sights, sounds, and smells of the enclaves and ghettos they are pledged to serve. They can see, for example, where city officials refuse to provide the services which are provided to other parts of the city, especially to the suburbs where the administrators live. The administrators can profit from experiencing the same feelings of uneasiness when they are in these communities as the students feel in the administrators' communities. Talking to the people in these communities will convince even the unsophisticated that the students who come to the college from these environments have special problems. One of the ways a visitor to depressed areas can judge the extent of his ignorance is to ask a member of that community to record each and every time the administrator makes an insensitive remark or asks a stupid question. Later, the administrator will be convinced that knowledge of one segment of the people he is serving is not one of his most admirable attributes. Visits to the public clinic, the local grocery store, and other areas of the indigent community can make the administrator further aware of at least one type of student with whom he has to deal.

Following this trip, the administrative team is ready for some academic and theoretical input. Consultants in sociology, psychology, and human relations from colleges and universities and from other agencies can add principles and explanations to the experiences that the conferees have had. These resource people can also assist the conference members in understanding themselves and their reactions.

Teachers cannot be forced to submit to this confrontation activity, but they should be invited to do so. Those who do not wish to take part should be excused. After all, teachers have been turned off by such sensitivity sessions in the past; and they have about been workshopped and retreated into insensitivity. Perhaps what is needed more is to provide teachers with more information. Those who do wish to take part may have essentially the same kind of experience as the administrators. And the administrators may go through the experience again with faculty members. The college senate and other such bodies can also be invited. Such bodies may be asked what actions should take place when acts of bigotry are substantiated against faculty members or administrators and to assist in the formulation of rules.

But workshops are not the only means for confronting bigotry in an institution. Anglo administrators rarely, if ever, join any organization or board that represents minority groups. They do join the Rotary, Kiwanis, Lions, and other such organizations; but the National Association for the Advancement of Colored People and the various Asian and other minority group organizations do not enjoy their membership. The upshot is that community college administrators follow the patterns of the rest of lower middle-class society. Just their membership and infrequent appearance in these organizations will add some credibility to their rhetoric of equality. Ninety-nine per cent of minority group organizations are not radical or controversial. Their members, for the most part, are professional and semiprofessional members of their communities. The administrator's job would not be threatened because of his participation with other ethnic groups; in fact, his job may become easier. One administrator notes in one breath, "Only about 4 or 5 per cent of our students are radical." In the next breath he says, "I would like to become a part of some of these minority group clubs and associations, but my more active students say that they are not militant enough or that they are too white." In other words, he is listening more to the 4 or 5 per cent than to the vast majority. These are the inconsistencies and illogical rationales nonwhites constantly observe in white administrators, why they do not respect many of them, and why they feel that administrators aid and abet much of the bigotry in their institutions. Yet the solution in this case, at least, is a very simple one.

Another aspect of this problem is discrimination in hiring. A considerable body of knowledge on dealing with this discrimination comes from such dedicated organizations as the Anti-Defamation League and the National Association for the Advancement of Colored People. Their guidelines can be summarized as follows: The board of trustees and top administrators should make a clear and unequivocal statement of policy on employing nonwhite personnel. After such a declaration, the administrators should inform employees, either directly or through their supervisors, that special efforts will be made to recruit minority group employees. In announcing this policy, administrators should not try to persuade present employees to accept minority groups. There is even some desirability in confronting employees with the fact of minority group hiring without prior information. Careful preparation of supervisors is essential, including holding sessions to help them anticipate and handle difficult situations.

Administrators should use the same care in selecting minority group persons as that which they use in selecting any other staff member; that is, they should look for people who appear to have potential for success. In addition to choosing the right people, the institution must work to ensure a gradual scattering of new minority group instructors and administrators among different departments, divisions, and so forth, filling vacancies as they occur and as applicants are able to qualify.

Absolute fairness and impartiality in dealing with problems introduced by nonwhites should be maintained, and clear enforcement of the changed policy and persistence in its execution must be preserved despite initial resistance. Besides refusing to tolerate any subterfuge on the part of supervisors, the administrator should be willing to deal strongly with interference, resistance, failure to cooperate, and policy violations. It does little good to appeal to the individuals and groups concerned on the basis of religious principles or brotherhood or American traditions of fair play and equality of justice, although these considerations should not be completely abandoned.

In short, a college, if it so chooses, can bring to bear the expertise of its faculty in spite of the normal conservatism of the group; the power and influence of its board of trustees; the skill of its administrators; the concern and talents of people in its community; and the energy, concern, and idealism of its student body to help in solving the problem of bigotry on campus. After (or if) all these things are done, bigotry will not be eliminated. If it is it would be an accident. But at least it will not exist because no attempts at action were taken.

Discrimination in education is as American as apple pie. Nowhere is the foregoing statement more apparent than in the community college. Lombardi (1969) writes:

Junior colleges are vulnerable to the charge of neocolonialism, i.e., that whites hold the positions of power, influence, and prestige, while blacks hold the menial or less influential positions. The few blacks who hold positions of power, influence, and prestige are considered tokens to the concept of equal opportunity employment practice. On the academic staffs, the colleges, while not as lily white as formerly, are still predominantly so. The proportion of black instructors is low, and the proportion of black administrators is lower.

124

New Recommendations for New Problems

Once an institution has begun to make breakthroughs in eliminating discrimination in hiring, it often finds that those non-whites who do become administrators have special problems with whites and with their own groups. What can be done to alleviate these problems? Let us begin by looking at what whites expect of nonwhite administrators. They expect them to be experts on everything nonwhite, even though nonwhite administrators constantly point out that members of any group of nonwhites are as different as members of any group of whites. These administrators are routinely asked about their acquaintance with every other member of their ethnic group in the whole community or city. If some problem or crisis situation erupts on the campus among members of his own group, the nonwhite administrator is asked to perform or to assist in performing jobs that the white deans are paid to do. Thus, the nonwhite administrators become the emissaries of and the mediators between the ethnic groups they represent and others in the college, even though they usually hold minor positions. They are called upon to assume the responsibilities of deans and presidents because the latter feel unqualified, unable, or afraid to intervene in such situations (although perhaps all three feelings are justified). And if nonwhites are in sharp disagreement or violent confrontation among themselves, the black administrators are routinely expected to go in and play John Wayne by settling the argument and, if necessary, by disarming the combatants. Only John Wayne can fight a whole tribe of Indians alone—and the Indians need help. One can see why nonwhite students say, in reference to blacks, that "whites do not want an ordinary black man, they want a supernigger."

Black administrators in particular resent this role of being the black in residence—an expert on everything colored black. Increasingly, they are resisting being the firemen in higher education. They realize, even if others do not, that they cannot walk on water. All of them freely accept the liaison and mediation functions when these functions are their responsibilities, but they resent being used. The idea lurks in their minds that as soon as the fires are out, those

125

who hired them will drop them just as quickly. Perhaps they were chosen for the wrong reasons in the first place.

If whites could attend a black caucus at some of the national and regional meetings and conventions, they would be amazed, shocked, and angered to hear some of the reports black administrators make before the caucus. They explain what happens to them at their home institutions. Some have positive reports to make; most, however, seem cynical and explain their reasons. These caucuses are positive activities; they provide an opportunity for the administrators to unburden themselves. If white administrators had the opportunity to hear these men and women talk for just ten minutes about how they are treated (professionally and socially), they would never make the trite, unrealistic, and untrue statement: "We don't have any problems at our institution." Attendance at one of these caucuses would be an education for many. The reporters are not irresponsible people raving with hot rhetoric; they are well educated men and women who are concerned about all students. Most whites will never visit one of these meetings because they cannot fulfill the prerequisite: be black. Yet, "Who would want to be that?" asked a young Oklahoman in a sensitivity training session in Chicago.

Nonwhite administrators have other complaints. Too often when they report to the campus for the first time, white administrators attempt to find them nonwhite secretaries and all of the other nonwhite fringe benefits "he may be happier with." This is the wrong way to go. Any nonwhite administrator who is his own man chooses his own secretary, whatever race she happens to be. He also chooses his own friends, community of residence (if he has a choice), social activities, and so forth. Whites trying to isolate him from white women, friends, communities, social activities, and the like only reveal their own hang-ups and bigotries.

There are other subtle (or obvious) behaviors of white administrators toward their black colleagues. One blond youngster who is a part-time student at a community college and a part-time attendant at the local golf course observed, "You know, I always see the white administrators together on Saturdays and sometimes

on Sundays down at the golf course. I never see the black administrator or faculty members. I happen to know that some of them
golf rather well. Aren't they ever invited?" "No," was the uncom-
plicated response from each of the blacks on the faculty and from the
one administrator. At the next bitch-in, a Black Student Union
member asked the white administrators why they excluded blacks
from their away-from-school activities such as golf. The administrators were told that they could plead the fifth. They chose to reply.
The following is an exact reproduction of a portion of their dialogue:

"I didn't know any of them played golf."

"Did you ask any one of them?"

"No."

The second man's response to the inquiry: "I thought they
would prefer playing with their own kind, er—er group, that is."

"What do you mean?"

"I mean other coloreds, that is, er blacks."

"Did you ask any one of them?"

"No I didn't. It's like I said. I thought they would be happier playing with their own buddies."

From the third respondent: "It wasn't prejudice. It's just
that nobody remembered to ask them."

"Nobody said it was prejudice. But how did the new white
members on the staff get to play in the group?"

"Okay, you've made your point."

"By the way, aren't you in charge of the human relations
program here?"

"I said, you've made your point."

Eight other responses were equally as defensive and insensitive. The lesson for white administrators is obvious. By being aware
and sensitive they can go a long way toward helping nonwhite
administrators resolve some of the special problems they face in
community colleges.

The administrator in the community college cannot expect
that other members of his administrative staff, as well as the teaching and classified staff, will not be blatant in their bigoted acts be-

cause they are supposed to be educated people. It is well demonstrated and documented that education and training have little effect on the attitudes of bigots (Allport, 1958).

It takes a well thought out and well developed program to fight bigotry on a campus with administrators who are strong enough to implement programs once they are evolved. Programs to fight or counteract bigotry start with the security officer on the parking lot, the guy who sweeps the floor, up through and including the chief administrative officer. It is with the total involvement of the entire staff that one can at least deal with the problem—even if he cannot solve it.

To sum up this discussion of white expectations of nonwhite administrators, whites are like all people. Some of them respect the nonwhite administrator for his ability and see him in relationship to how well he does his job. When he does that job well, they say so to him and to others. When he does not do the job well they say so only to him. The great compliment that can be paid a white administrator by a black one is: "He's straight."

Nonwhites also have expectations of nonwhite administrators that the administrators cannot always fulfill and that therefore give them additional problems. Those who are looking for teaching positions and other jobs expect him to be able to provide them with employment and frequently expect him to go outside of prescribed policies, procedures, and channels to accomplish this goal. Like their white counterparts, nonwhite businessmen, legislators, social club members, fraternity brothers, sorority sisters, golfing friends, old family friends, militants, union officials, civil rights officials, and many others call on the black administrator. They ask, demand, request, extort, threaten, and apply other coercion and persuasion to make him respond to their respective needs. They ask for employment, endorsement, support, membership, financial contributions to every affair and event in the community, participation in programs, speeches, and so forth. Some people simply call him up or walk in off the street to ask his advice. Because he is usually more accessible, perhaps more students (black and white) talk to the black administrator than to any other administrator on campus. Almost a thousand community college presidents may deny this latter statement, but, then, they do not have black administrators on their campuses.

Some nonwhite students expect the administrator, as "a brother," to get them registered late, a loan or scholarship, into a class which has been closed, a refund, a grade changed, and so forth. Some students want to "borrow" money from him. Others ask him to discriminate against white students in order to get students from his own ethnic group in the college. They are quick to point out that whites have always practiced discrimination and still do, and they are right. The administrator is certainly tempted to discriminate, and some probably do. Yet, little can be accomplished, in the long run, either for himself or for black students, if the black administrator wraps himself in the same shroud of bigotry as the white community college "dealer" who preceded him or who is his coworker.

In urban areas, nonwhite groups want to use college resources since the community college is supposed to belong to the community. Too often, many of those in the ethnic communities expect the administrator not only to make sure that a facility or a college resource is available to them but also to absorb or to underwrite any costs incurred. Sometimes this can be done; most often, it cannot.

Nonwhites frequently want to know whether "their representative" in the college has any power and constantly check to see for themselves whether he does. If the administrator has power, they want to determine how much, and they want to see it demonstrated periodically. If he has no power, they consider him as being on a treadmill. Although he is not always condemned, he is definitely not respected. If he does not have the authority he should have because he fails to demand it and take it, then the community has contempt for him. These are not do-nothing times in the community college. Lethargy in their representatives is less and less an acceptable response with the nonwhite community. They will no longer accept a black front man, for example, or one with a "white mentality."

Black incompetents are like white incompetents; they are burdens to an institution and detrimental to the welfare of students. They always want to step outside of the procedures to get employment. Once hired, they cry loudest for tenure and the other safeguards which protect them from exposure. When they are not a member of the college staff, they use the energy, anger, idealism, and genuine concern of students to foster their own causes. If they are part-time teachers and want to be full-time ones, probationary and want to be regular, temporary and want to be permanent, they use the students, the unrest, their class time, community scandal sheets, and outside militant groups who listen to them to support their causes. Black militants have only contempt for these incompetents. They accuse them of pimping on the revolution.

The black community does not have many heroes in higher education, many who have made it, who can hold their own academically, socially, and professionally with any group. For example, fewer than five thousand blacks in the United States hold the Ph.D. degree. As a consequence, when they find someone to act as their spokesman, they want him to be academically pure both to keep those people quiet who would question his qualification and because higher education is psychotic about credentials. But more important, the black administrator must be strong—stronger than his white counterpart—because he has tougher battles to fight. He must indeed find ways to respond to all those persons we mentioned above who make demands of him.

How can a nonwhite administrator handle these demands? Minority administrators know that while white incompetents may expect to get jobs and other considerations, their own communities as a whole do not appear to have such expectations for them. All their communities want to know is that when there is an opportunity in the offing or when an action is taken against a member of their group, they will have equal access to the opportunity and they will be treated fairly when there is a problem. It is the re-

130

sponsibility of a nonwhite administrator to monitor this process as best he can. The education community needs to be aware that when a minority incompetent is found in their midst, he should be so advised by the appropriate administrator, not necessarily the nonwhite one of the same ethnic group, unless it is his job. The nonwhite administrator must be honest even when it means that his decisions or actions may hurt someone in his community. Regarding the problem of proving his power, he displays an undesirable image when he plays administrator with those in his community who ask for his help. If he cannot fulfill a request, he should say so and not make people return to his office or make numerous telephone calls for information, assistance, and positions which he does not have the authority or resources to provide. The administrator cannot play the role of politician with this community by telling the people how wonderful he is and how much he has done. The evidence of his importance comes from the community itself. If he is anybody important to them, they know who he is. If he has accomplished anything worth noting, it is already known and appreciated. There is no need for curtain calls.

Although whites seem to be impressed with job titles and other such designations of importance, blacks tend not to be. They know that titles bestowed upon or earned by the members of their group have not, in the past, made a significant difference between themselves and the titleholders. The nonwhite administrator knows when he has pleased and won the respect of his community. They talk about him in the barber shop, they wave at him from passing cars, gardeners ask to do his lawn, his wife is protected when attending a meeting in the ghetto, he is better known than the college president (if he is not the president). Newspaper clippings of his statements are on bulletin boards of high schools, pool halls, restaurants, churches, recreation centers, and the like. Once accepted, he becomes a model for the community, accepted by moderate and militant, the educated and illiterate.

Another problem of major magnitude for the administrator in the community college, especially for the president, is dealing with the business officer. The business manager is a key person in transactions between the college and architects, auditors, state and government officers, vendors, and chancellors or district presidents, as well as all the other people who have business with the college. This is one of the most important areas in the college, and he is an essential person in the organization. But college business managers are notorious for not confining their talents and influence within the parameters of their position.

A weak president and a strong business manager have ruined many an education program. One group of authors (Blocker and others, 1965) put it this way:

> *It is axiomatic that control of college finances means control of the educational program. In all too many instances fiscal officers have exerted undue influence upon the program through their control of the funds necessary for its development and implementation. It should not be the responsibility of the business manager to allocate funds in specific amounts to particular activities of the college; unfortunately, there are far too many situations in which the business manager does just this. Requests for funds are channeled through the business office, and the decision regarding such requests too often is made by the business manager or by members of his staff. Such staff members are the custodians of college funds; their responsibility is to safeguard monies and to perform services—e.g., accounting, purchasing, contracting—designed to support and implement the educational programs of the college. Another problem is the domination of budget development by the business manager. Budgets should originate with the departments and should be reviewed by the president and the deans of the various divisions. After the allocations of monies for various purposes have been agreed upon by these administrative officers, it is the responsibility of the business manager to implement the decisions. The business manager should not be permitted to make decisions which would alter or nullify the meaning and purposes of the original budget.*

In multicampus districts, the activities of business officers can allow one campus' becoming a showcase college because it receives a disproportionately larger share of the funds. In some cases even the district president does not know the fiscal condition of the district. Since purchasing agents answer to the business manager, it is not at all unusual to find that the appropriate campus person (dean, division chairman) approves of an item to be purchased only to have the order held up by the district business officer even after the local campus business manager has cleared it. It is also common to find that an item has been changed because the purchasing agent found it cheaper and did not bother to inform the campus which initiated the purchase order.

In many other situations a college president finds that a business officer is making educational decisions. In a midwestern college, the financial officer decides educational programs, and the college president seems powerless to do anything about it. The president could change this situation, but he represents those college heads who lose their authority through inaction; as a result, others assume his responsibility.

A weak president who has a strong financial officer also has many morale problems as others on the staff discover that he permits the business officer to make educational decisions, thus overruling his instruction and student personnel divisions in deference to his financial officer. The president who gives his word and then retracts it after consultation with the business officer also blurs the lines of authority so that decision makers do not always know their roles. People three and four levels down in the hierarchy may effectively reverse a decision made by the president; or they can effectively make the decision by not taking action on certain requests for purchases. When the business manager is strong, presidents in multicampus districts hesitate to make decisions. They hesitate because they never know whether their decisions will be reversed once they reach the central office; they know that it can be routine for a campus decision to be countermanded without explanation; they know that sometimes the situation can get so bad that they must diplomatically ask the chancellor to put everything in writing. Obviously, such a district head lacks credibility with his administrators. As a consequence, when the chancellor makes a verbal

133

commitment to his campus administrators which is not in writing, some go back to their offices and write him memoranda using the following language: "Pursuant to our conversation regarding . . ., it is my understanding that . . . If my understanding is essentially correct, I will proceed as of this date. . . . This memorandum, therefore, will confirm our arrangement." This is one technique used to get around the actions of the business officer and the tendency of the president or chancellor to reverse his decisions.

This problem of the business officer however is one of the easier ones to solve. Two well designed manuals, one for policies and one for procedures, should be developed to clearly define what the business officer's (and every other administrator's) role and responsibility are. For every policy in the manual there should be a corresponding procedure in the procedures manual. When the business officer gets out of line, he ought to be told so. When he does not do what he is hired to do, he should be replaced—but only after he has had an opportunity to improve. His interference with the area of responsibility of another administrator without invitation should not be tolerated. And any president who permits this interference to continue once it is brought to his attention should be given the opportunity to resign along with the business officer. Many presidents and business officers would be looking for jobs if boards of trustees would take the foregoing seriously—and they should. A change in presidents and business officers periodically would probably be a good thing for community college education. This does not mean that presidents should be dismissed indiscriminately every four or five years. It does mean that they ought not to remain in the job so long that the president begins to call the institution "my school," and the business officer behaves as though the fiscal resources belong to him. Interim leaves, in which the administrator could go back to school or travel and look at other institutions, may be a solution to keeping administrators first rate.

Like the business manager, the faculty also want to be involved in all facets of the community college. No one would question that faculty must plan programs and courses and assist in planning and developing facilities. These areas are not the current extent of faculty involvement and interest however. As in the past, faculty insist on monopolizing the hiring and assessment of other faculty. And now many of them also insist on having a controlling voice in all areas of the institution. Let us examine this latter demand first.

Administrators, especially the president, are responsible (or are the scapegoats) for everything that goes wrong in the institution; and they should be. But as faculty members make increasingly unrealistic demands and engage increasingly in unprofessional behavior, it seems that only the administrators are expected to play by the old rules of conduct and behavior, attempt to apply reason, and keep their heads cool although their stomachs are being eaten away. As faculties demand and receive decision-making power in many areas of the institution, administrators agree that the worst problem they have to contend with "is the increasing authority of faculty (and students) with no increase in responsibility, and, at the same time, the lessening of authority of the president with no change in his responsibility" (Linowitz and others, 1970).

It is no secret: Administrators feel that dealing with faculty is one of the most difficult areas in higher education. It is not student activism, as many might have imagined. The American Council on Education has attempted to determine those particular issues which bothered college presidents and other administrators most. Administrators were asked to state the "worst one or two problems which create or increase tension on your campus."

Leading the tallies is the faculty: many respondents mention this constituent as one or another source of difficulties. . . . One president complains of the "unwillingness or inability of the faculty to adjust to change," another of "suffocating academic arrogance." While a number of presidents see the faculty as the entrenched voice of conservatism on the campus, others are disturbed by the active role of faculty in promoting dissent and divisiveness. One is vexed by "faculty members who encourage students, by positive efforts or lack of enough guts to oppose, in their efforts to politicize the [college]." Another notes that tenured faculty are participating in "whispered harassment of the president and his office (or other administrative offices) by SDS-type student groups."

In like manner, the subjects of the above study criticized faculty "for their persistent unwillingness . . . to involve students in some of their hallowed preserves." The administrators agreed that there is a "confusion of roles in the performance of responsibilities." They were also disenchanted with important decisions being made without consultation with them, although one said, "Consultation is grinding us to a halt."

I am not saying that faculty should not be involved in policy formulation. The logic of their positions and the nature of their task dictate otherwise. But faculty do not have any more inherent right to be involved than does any other group, including administrators, students, secretaries, and custodians. My view here departs from the old European concept and tradition of what higher education and the community of scholars should be. But the European model changed the day it was imported; furthermore, that tradition was spawned in the Middle Ages and the Middle Ages were not exactly a time of enlightenment.

Regarding the faculty prerogative of recruiting and assessing other faculty members, I cannot concede that only they can do it competently. Faculties are conservative. The evidence indicates that they resist innovation (Evans, 1967). When they control the hiring and firing in an institution, they have exclusionary and discriminatory policies. Teaching applicants who represent a different race or religion or espouse a different set of ideas do not get jobs. Faculties also perpetuate inbreeding, which is one of the ways they preserve tradition—the wrong traditions. Young teachers who are full of new ideas and energy but who are not tenured are not allowed to rock the boat. A power-centered faculty is usually more self-centered than student-centered, more concerned with the subject matter than with the needs of the institution and society. Unlimited authority and control and power in the hands of any particular group have serious deficiencies. Whether that group happens to be faculty or otherwise it should not have the exclusive right to deny others input into decisions and policy. The board of trustees is the only group which may have that right by law.

Faculty members insist that only they can evaluate other faculty members. Almost any other person in the institution is probably more aware of the kind of instruction taking place in the teacher's classroom than are his colleagues. Students are especially aware. They inform the counselors, other students, their parents, and advisers about the quality of a specific man's instruction, although none of these listeners, with the exception of an occasional angry student, accepts the responsibility to tell an administrator (he never tells the teacher himself) that his teacher is incompetent. A professor's colleagues are rarely honest enough to tell him, even when such a revelation can serve as constructive criticism. Moore (1970b) asked 403 teachers in twenty-six community colleges about the teaching of their colleagues. All said that their coworkers were doing a fine job. Yet, 391 of the teachers had never visited the classroom of a colleague to watch him teach and had never seen his course outline or syllabi; 83 per cent of the teachers did not know whether the colleagues in their department had any publications. Vocational and community service teachers knew more about the abilities of their fellow teachers than did college transfer instructors. An overwhelming 98 per cent of the teachers in the college parallel area said that not even their division chairman visited their classroom to observe after the completion of the first year of teaching. Eight out of ten teachers of transfer students did not feel that the division or department chairman could evaluate them or their teaching. Conversely, the exact same ratio of vocational teachers and 76 per cent of the community service instructors felt that they could be evaluated by not only their supervisor but also by the students and others. Teachers in all divisions suspected the competence of some of their fellow faculty members, but the general feeling was that this was the administrator's problem, not a problem for members of the faculty.

In dealing with faculty demands for the exclusive right to hire and fire their colleagues and for control over policy in other areas, the administrator has two problems: to involve faculty so that they can best serve the students, the institution, and themselves; and to be sure their involvement is shared with others in the institution. Perhaps what is needed is to have the roles of the different human inputs of the college community (faculty, administration, board of trustees, and students) better defined. The current trend, through negotiations in some cases and the university tradition in others, is to place the control of the college in the hands of faculty and the responsibility for it on the shoulders of administrators. This has the net effect of producing chaos. One group has the control and the safeguards (tenure, guarantees against dismissal, no audit of competence, negotiation rights, and so on), while the other has the responsibility and no safeguards. I believe this position is an unhealthy one for administrators just as is their own perpetual facade to the public that everything is fine in the institution whether it is or not. To say one thing in the presence of faculty, to the media, and before other public forums about the importance of faculty involvement and about their dedication and competence and another thing in private to their fellow administrators must create severe conflict for many. One responsibility of administration today is to make sure that everybody knows the problems and benefits of faculty involvement. Faculties will have more to say about what happens in the college than they now do. The question is whether administrators will help to guide, direct, and influence this involvement or will simply complain about it.

Inevitably the community college administrator will be called upon to open the educational process in his institution to public audit. This new approach to accountability indicates a shift in emphasis. Instead of measuring our services in terms of what is taught, it measures our services in terms of what students learn. Our fellow citizens expect educators to significantly raise the percentage of our students who succeed not only in the classroom but also in life. If curricular and instructional change are needed so that this will happen, they expect educators to take the initiative to make those changes. For the administrator to do nothing is to create a further crisis of public confidence in education.

New Recommendations for New Problems

Accountability is such an important issue in community college education that the American Association of Junior Colleges convention was opened on March 1, 1971, with a congressional panel on "The 1970's: Accountability and the Congressional View." Two Senators—Robert A. Taft, Ohio, and Alan Cranston, California—and two Representatives—Parren J. Mitchell, Maryland, and Albert H. Quie, Minnesota—were the panelists.

Accountability is another area of faculty-administrative conflict. People who cannot define it discuss it. Some educational and professional journals (*Kappan*, 1970) devote whole issues to the subject, replete with theories and research models demonstrating how accountability can be accomplished. Other journals (*Changing Education*, 1969) suggest that it should be rejected at all cost. Nixon in his 1970 message on educational reform and outstanding educational personalities (Harcleroad, 1970; McGill, 1971) consistently reminded educators of the need for accountability.

Although responsibility is one of the qualities educators hope to instill in young people, they are frequently the outstanding exemplars in resisting it when it applies to themselves. In fact, two-year college people have taken on some of the worst habits of four-year college and university people with regard to performance appraisal. It is understandable, therefore, why foundations and the American public—through legislators and boards of trustees—are calling on educators to assess their educational performance and to devise methods for correcting malfunctions (see Davies, 1970; Elam, 1970; Lessinger, 1970a, 1970b, 1970c, 1970d; Meade, 1968; Millett, 1970; Rhodes, 1970; Roueche and Baker, 1970; Roueche and others, 1971; Schwartz, 1970).

Such accountability is taboo, a no-no, among educators. When some suggest that teachers should establish work objectives and be measured according to those objectives, many teachers yell foul, and the union echoes. They claim that performance criteria are nothing but a scheme to weed out teachers who do not conform and to force other teachers to stay in line through a system of rewards and punishments rigged in favor of those who are best at following orders. Teachers point out that such performance cri-

139

teria are sinister weapons to combat their efforts to manage their profession. They want to develop their own criteria and establish their own standards, with no outside input. This practice should not be permitted. Administrators who are charged with the supervision of instruction, students who are taught, and those who pay the bill must have some input. Just as faculties ask for input into every phase of the college, so should persons other than faculty have their say about what is taught, why, to what ends, and who should do it.

The effectiveness of such an evaluation program depends on the attitude and the skills of the supervisory personnel. In fact, accountability should begin with the president, dean of instruction, and other top administrators. They should demonstrate that they, too, are willing to be evaluated. At Seattle Central Community College the administrative staff instituted such an evaluation program. Each administrator, including the president, writes his own objectives for the year and sends copies to the other administrators. At the end of the year, each makes a written report indicating the degree to which he has accomplished his goals. Also recorded in the report are conferences attended, publications if any, community contacts and speeches, visits in the community, outreach activities, and so forth. All the reports are bound in a single document, and each administrator receives a copy of the document for his files. The intent is to see that additional copies are routed through the faculty as an information item only. Now that it has been demonstrated that such a program is viable, the faculty will be asked to take part in the evaluation of the administration by indicating the criteria which should be included in the evaluation instrument. Thoughtful professionals are indicating positive interest and concern. There is no evaluation mechanism for faculty. Perhaps the attitude of the administration will suggest to the faculty that such a program can be a positive force in the institution. There are two-year colleges currently involved in the accountability concept in both theory and practice: John Tyler Community College, Brookdale Community College, Moraine Valley Community College,

140

Kittrell College, Mitchell Junior College, and Mount Olive Junior College are examples.

Lack of administration and faculty evaluation is irresponsible behavior on the part of both groups and the board of trustees. In community colleges with no faculty evaluation policies or practice, the only written data in the faculty member's (or administrator's) personnel file are his transcript, original application, placement on the salary schedule, credits earned and forwarded, and so on. Yet, when this member chooses to go to another job or college or wants to be considered for promotion within the same structure, there is not an anecdotal record in his file. The references he asks for come off the top of the head of his current division/department chairman, are ad-libbed by people judging his personality rather than his ability to teach or administer. There are sound reasons for evaluations. They can be used to reward, commend, provide assistance to, and identify potential among the staff. The administrator must support the premise that the college—all facets of the college—must answer to the people.

Resistance to such evaluation, however, has been reflected in professional negotiations. Increasingly, we see included in bargaining proposals guarantees to prevent evaluation. Such guarantees are among the evils inherent in the bargaining process for academic professionals. In fact, no single event or group of events has affected community colleges for good and ill in quite the way professional negotiations have and will in the future. Much of the good we have yet to see, with the exception of improved welfare in terms of salary and fringe benefits.

As a result of negotiation laws, a few serious problems have arisen, and their nature seems to have crystalized with sufficient clarity so that the first amendments to the original bills or laws should now be considered. Present laws require that faculty have the right to meet, confer, and negotiate with the local board on an almost unlimited range of issues, including what have traditionally been management decisions in such areas as utilization of staff, staff assignments, and selection of the administrators. These issues also include salaries, salary schedules, fringe benefits, work load, and myriad other things.

Negotiation on these issues has been interpreted by some to mean either almost endless debate between the board and a faculty committee—and it is often considered a breach of faith if the board finally acts after months of negotiations—or requirements for reaching "agreement" on an issue before the board can act at all. The result of the first interpretation is that hundreds and hundreds of hours of faculty time are devoted to developing a case against or delaying board action on matters that affect them. Equally as much administrative time is spent developing postures to counteract faculty efforts. The faculty and administrative time, money, and resources spent are many times greater than those required for reasonable involvement and participation in the decision-making process of the college. This process takes the faculty and the administrators away from the student-related duties for which they are hired. (A partial work stoppage can go on almost continually.) As a result of the second interpretation, management decisions which may affect faculty—such as those dealing with work load or evaluation of performance—become almost impossible for a board to enact.

The present laws should be amended to separate those issues on which the faculty has the right to meet and confer with the local board from those issues on which they have a right to negotiate. The right to negotiate should be guaranteed for changes in salaries and salary schedules, fringe benefits such as health programs, sabbaticals, and leave programs, and other specific benefits. Items on which the faculty should have the right to *meet and confer* should include hiring and assignment practices, in-service training, curriculum, textbook selection, and other matters which relate to their input in the selection, performance, and evaluation of the faculty itself.

Who negotiates? This is another part of the problem. With present laws the local board or a committee thereof must negotiate with representatives of the faculty organization. But local trustees have personal responsibilities which prevent them from engaging in this activity as knowledgeably as they might. It may be more reasonable therefore for boards of trustees to be able to delegate this responsibility to a professional negotiator.

Impasse advisory committees are another problem under present negotiation laws. Such a committee now consists of several persons (appointed by an appointing authority) who are completely detached from the campus or district in which they are called. They usually include faculty and board members from other colleges or districts and sometimes a college president. They too often seek to find some middle ground between the faculty and the board and then recommend that the parties agree to their terms. The local board may have already made concessions that strain the budget to the maximum; offered salary increases higher than the legislature appropriated the funds to pay; and cut back on new programs, new equipment, or additional staff in such a way as to diminish the quality (to students) of the education program. Still, the impasse advisory committee usually urges the parties to seek agreement on some middle ground beyond the concessions already made.

The committee should have its purpose redefined. Its role, it would seem, should be to determine whether the local board negotiated with the authorized faculty organization under reasonable circumstances and for a sufficient time; whether the local board provided salary increases that comply with the intent of the legislature or made a judicious effort to do so or had a justifiable reason for failure to do so; and whether the local board complied with all other laws in providing benefits and services to the local faculty, such as health insurance, or had a justifiable reason for failure to do so.

In addition, at the present time, the appointing authority has no discretionary powers to determine whether there is a reasonable basis for the appointment of such a committee and for paying the costs of committee activity. A solution is to authorize the appointing authority to recognize as an impasse situation only those

143

where the appealing organization provides evidence of noncompliance by the board to the provisions of one of the laws cited above or violation of the intent of the legislature.

In other areas of negotiation, the administrator cannot count on changes in the law to protect his position; he must be strong himself. No word seems to frighten the administrator like the word *strike*. This is a tool of labor and a natural part of the bargaining process. It is, therefore, irresponsible for an administrator to capitulate each time a strike is threatened or occurs. If and when a strike does occur, under no circumstances should management or the board offer more to get those who withheld their services back to work than its best offer prior to the work stoppage. Strikes make believers of us all. We cannot afford them. People get behind in their mortgage payments, car notes, and other bills; they are unable to make anticipated purchases, plan trips, and must forego luxuries. If the strike lasts long enough nothing is gained by either side except a lesson in credibility. It becomes an absurd irrationality and the real losers are the students.

Mayors and blue ribbon committees increasingly attempt to influence the adversaries to go back to the bargaining table to establish some middle ground. But if there is no middle ground within the limits of fiscal responsibility or sound educational practice, the administrators should not agree to or endorse such a position or compromise. They and the board of trustees know more about the institution and its resources than any committee of outstanding citizens or mayor who is trying to keep the political heat off his back.

A faculty member on strike is a new and strange phenomenon in the academic community, and the present rules allow him to behave in irresponsible ways. But faculty do have a professional responsibility to the students. If the struck course or program is a prerequisite to others, the student has been placed at a disadvantage. He loses time and money and is delayed in getting his education. In such cases the student should be encouraged to sue the bargaining agent or the institution or both. If teachers are going to strike, it is only reasonable to have them strike prior to a quarter

144

or semester, rather than after it begins and students have committed their finances and time to the institution.

In the black community, a strike among community college teachers is considered "white folks' business." Many blacks do not support them. A work stoppage at a Chicago college is a case in point. According to one parent who had a student attending this college:

> *Our students won't lose much if they strike and stay out six months because they don't get much when they are not on strike. Unions don't strike to get more blacks or Mexicans or Puerto Ricans teaching at the college; they don't strike to weed out those teachers that ain't worth a damn; they don't strike to make that bureaucracy downtown any easier to deal with; and they don't strike to change all that academic bull they're teaching. Most of them teachers would be happy to come in at twelve o'clock, have an hour for lunch, and go home. Then, at the end of the year, ask for a sabbatical so they can have some time to rest the next year with pay. I will never vote for another levy. You know white folks all over this country have been voting against all these levies and taxes, and they get the most benefit out of them. It's about time black folks did the same; I know I am.*

There are many other people who share this mother's feelings. In Chicago, black organizations actively opposed a teachers' strike (*Newsweek,* January 25, 1971), and a group of whites also established counter picket lines.

Another threat of educational organizations is the sanction, whereby they say to the academic world that a specific college is not a good place to work because it failed to take certain actions proposed or supported by the organization. Sanctions are supposed to dissuade teachers, especially the very competent and well known ones, from taking teaching positions in the sanctioned college and to encourage those who are already teaching at the college to leave unless the institution shapes up. At this time, a sanction is little more than a slap on the wrist because of the surplus of teachers, including Ph.D.s. Even before the teacher surplus, however, the sanction was a threat only to administrators who were more concerned about the image of their institutions than about education.

When negotiations end, the theorizers suggest that everyone from both sides of the bargaining table should go back to doing a good job of educating young people. This suggestion is unrealistic regardless of how much it is desired. Each side tends to spend time monitoring the other. A union cannot remain in business unless it continues to demonstrate to its membership that the administration is capricious, is unresponsive, and is attempting to break the agreement. At the present time, harmony between faculty and administration is not one of the results that can be anticipated from the collective bargaining process. The adversary process between faculties and administration in higher education will deepen and harden for some time to come unless the public gets wise to the fact that its interest is not being protected. Eventually, adminstrators will become more skilled in the negotiating process than they now are, perhaps after there is nothing else to concede; and faculty will learn that responsibility accompanies academic freedom, financial increases, fringe benefits, and policy-making gains. But thus far, the creativity that can emerge out of the bargaining process has not emerged.

It may appear that this commentary has been particularly harsh in a book on administration. This harshness was intended. The image of faculty—like the image of the physician—is no longer one of service and commitment, and it should be. Both groups are pictured as greedy, money-grubbing, self-interested people who are not concerned with the needs of the people they are supposed to serve. In education, failure to meet these needs has bred suspicion of educators and has caused too many people to lose faith in the education process.

The excellence of an institution cannot exceed that of its faculty. Yet, excellence in the faculty is not prescribed by the number of degreed professionals on the staff and the other traditional criteria. In the contemporary community college, excellence should be measured in professionalism, dedication, and commitment. When

146

the big idea is replaced by the big buck; when the search for control becomes more important than the search for knowledge; when academic freedom becomes license for irresponsibility; when the degreed teachers in English literature become more important than the journeymen teachers of automotive mechanics; when the closed shop is the method by which one group of educators attempts to force all their peers to hold the same ideas; when the power to veto becomes more important than the desire to agree; when students become the pawns in the political games between the forces in the college, then the group proposing such ideas should be called back to sanity because professionalism, dedication, and commitment are not in evidence. And this criticism refutes the concept of the faculty as I wrote about it in *1970–71 The Year of the Faculty*, a publication in tribute to a community college faculty:

I see a faculty as many things: advisor and interrogator, exemplar and tutor, confidant and adversary, planner and innovator. And, a faculty is many job titles: philosopher and plumber, machinist and mathematician, baker and biologist. It is all colors, religions, and political persuasions. Most of all, I see a faculty as people— human beings with faces and ideas. As one observes these faces and encounters these ideas, he sees a group of educational practitioners cull wisdom from the concerns of students and evolve a new consensus of what the partnership in learning must be. He is sensitive to each faculty member's efforts to teach each of his students to question, to love, to live, to work, to strive, to be himself. He listens to the faculty listen. He observes how particular teachers have mastered the art and maturity of keeping little things little. He watches the faculty member who recognizes the cynic and the conformist in his classroom and deals with these two students as the imposters they are. Yet, the teacher does not judge, but examines. He accepts all of his students: housewife and minister, philanthropist and militant. Most important, the good teacher takes the student who has forgotten to dream and the one who never learned, and teaches them both how. And, this, after all, is what a faculty is all about.

The logic of their association would preclude the continued adversarial relationship between faculty and administrators.

Closely related to the problem of negotiation is politics. Boards of trustees do not have a lobby to protect the public. As a result, we are beginning to see administrators behave like legislators.

Administrators act as though they are running for political office. They do not offend the left by supporting the right; or the middle by supporting either persuasion. They become experts at saying nothing, politicians rather than statesmen, failing to realize that saying nothing does support one side. Whether this course is due to naivete or shrewdness is subject to speculation; the fact remains that our administrators are rapidly becoming sensitive to special interest groups both within and outside of the college. In some communities, they sell out the needs of some students in order to support the athletic program, trade away a part of the vocational program to provide shorter working hours for the college parallel division, and so forth. The administrator compromises, trades, gives and takes, involves himself in what-for-what swapping to the extent that what is best for the education of the student is sometimes lost in the process. His credibility is lost with many people in the same process.

It is common to hear administrators publicly claim to be in favor of equal employment but privately refuse to take a position on the Joint Apprenticeship Committees and their exclusionary practices in assigning apprentices to his college. He does what he has to do. He makes sure that what he does is politically sound if not educationally sound. Better the former than the latter. If he feels that the public wants repression, he represses. He corrupts the language with ambiguity. So often he is a man on the way up meeting a man on the way down. To the man descending, he is a threat. And to the man going up, he is an obstacle. He is frequently so busy with self that he fails to tell legislators that they are making laws which are totally inappropriate for an educational institution. Although he knows that it is not uncommon for a politician to sell out his constituency for a special-interest group, too often he too sells out his special-interest group—the students. He sells out to the demands of many pressure groups, partially because it is easier to join the adversary than to fight him. Perhaps a course on how to deal with legislators should be included in administrative training.

To end this chapter on solutions to administrative problems, I make here some suggestions for improving community relations since no area is more important for the administrator to master than his ability to work with the public. The role of the community college administrator is an expanding one. He has become essential to his community. Not only does he lead and direct the instructional program, but he must also interpret the total college program, as well as his own function, to the community and gain understanding and support for it.

To develop effective community relations the community college administrator should put together a handbook of facts on the community. The most immediate and practical value of the handbook is to have useful information assembled in one convenient source. But the greatest benefits of the book are the intangible ones. While the specific data change, the insights gained in the process of getting the information help the administrator establish effective communications as an educator and community leader.

The administrator should secure most of this information himself. Much data can be obtained from directories of local and state governmental and of social agencies; some have to be obtained by personal contact. The following kinds of data are essential.

First, the community college administrator must make many decisions based on knowledge of the educational levels of the persons of voting age within the district where his college is located. He should know such demographic information as the percentage of persons who did not attend beyond elementary school, did not attend beyond high school, and attended beyond high school. This kind of information provides him with some enrollment and recruitment data as well as support information based on voting characteristics of his constituency. He also wants to know the employment and housing patterns of his campus area. All this information should be placed in a loose-leaf binder in outline form (see Guide, p. 155) so that the busy administrator can read it at a glance.

Second, the administrator must determine as well as he can the ethnic composition of his school and the community he serves. He should take special note of holidays and days of other special observance, know the birth dates of special heroes, be aware of the impact these days or events might have on his institution, and read the small community ethnic newspapers. Special interest groups such as the National Association for the Advancement of Colored People, the Japanese-American Citizens' League, the Jewish Community Council operate within the community college service area. The administrator should compile a list with the name of each organization, its purposes, meeting place, leader, and address.

Third, a community college exists in a public and political environment. The administrator should have immediately available the number of registered voters. It is to his advantage to know and list each political district and precinct in the college service area. The Senators and Congressmen, the state senators and representatives, the city council members or aldermen, the committee men and committee women, the elected or appointed office holders (current or past), the precinct captains, and other such political animals should be listed also. In his handbook, the administrator should write their names, political parties, office and home addresses and telephone numbers, occupations prior to election (one day one of these people may agree to serve on an advisory group), years their terms expire, and districts they represent. The administrator also should know where the political parties have their headquarters and meeting places and which other people are also active in the political structure, such as block captains and clerks in various offices of the city and state. It is important that the administrator understand the political organization of the district in which his college is located, including the dominant political party and the key individuals in each party. This information should also include personal impressions of the organization as a force in the community. Obviously, every administrator should not be expected to know every person or all the data mentioned above. He should know, however, those persons who may in one way or another affect his particular area.

Fourth, usually the administrator gets to know the tradesmen and professional persons (physicians, attorneys) who, because of their occupational status, are influential within the community. The community college person needs to quickly learn which conditions beyond occupational status contribute to their influence and what other people have strong influence and power in the community. In some communities the informal leadership is as important as the formal one. In every community the busybody can frequently alert the administrator to more about the distribution of power in five minutes free than paid resource people can uncover in six months. In addition, some people who live outside the immediate community have influence within it. Labor groups are a case in point. Welfare agencies which send New Careers, Manpower Development Training Act, and Division of Vocational Rehabilitation students to the college may have some influence. It helps to know who the people are in these agencies.

Fifth, the voting history of the community is another piece of valuable information. The administrator can find these data at election offices and in newspaper offices and can then record them on separate pages (see Guide).

There is little value in additional narrative here. Every administrator knows or quickly learns the valuable information he must have if he is to serve his community effectively (see Guide for examples).

Good public relations is a typical and traditional problem of community colleges. It is like the improvement of instruction—one of the most significant and least accomplished administrative goals in the college. Regardless of his problems the administrator must remember his student body. The majority of the students have most of the characteristics of the disadvantaged: They are fighting for their lives and losing. They are high-risk, they were average or below average as high school students, and they have not changed their habits when they enter as freshmen. These stu-

151

dents come from homes where they are the first generation to go to college (Knoell, 1970; Cross, 1968). Their parents, in many cases, have been hostile to formal education. The students have been dropouts and flunkouts. Their goals have been unrealistic, ill-defined, and they want immediate gratification of their needs. Some of the students are from affluent homes but are, nonetheless, academically high-risk. Earlier, we described a number of minority students. They are not middle-class. They represent the other side of the comparison: suburbs and slums—they are from the slums; rich and poor—they are the poor; white and nonwhite—they are the black, Chicano, Native American. People who give them instruction reflect an attitude of low expectations. Minority group or lower-class students, as it were, have always rejected the unreality of the curriculum. Their major complaints have been that the curriculum fails to illuminate social realities, meet individual needs, and develop humane values. For them, compensatory education has not obtained hoped-for results. They have been pointing out that it is impossible for them to evolve a perception of personal worth when they are bombarded with alienating, divisive, disillusioning experiences inside the institution that purports to democratize them. For them, we have not seen any improvement in their education. It is not that we do not know what to do. Rather, we have not done what we need to do, particularly those who have direct contact with students.

In conclusion let me sum up the administrator's situation and his options as I see them. When administrators fail to provide the services in an institution, when they become more concerned about prestige than people, when they accept that which is educationally unsound to keep the peace, when they are not committed to accountability, when their statements on the open door are only public relations rhetoric, and when they are not open, candid, and free of subterfuge, then they should be prepared to move—or be moved.

What is greatly needed is to clearly define what an administrator's job is, the role he is expected to play, the authority he has, and his areas of responsibility. It borders on lunacy to give a man a job and the responsibility for carrying it out, and then to strip him of the authority to perform it. It is equally as irresponsible to expect an administrator to be a good decision maker when he must first ask the constituencies (board of trustees, community, faculty, and students) whether they accept his decision. If faculty senates and other committees are going to make the decisions, then they too should be held responsible when something goes wrong and when heads must roll. If tenure were suspended while individuals held offices on important decision-making committees and if it were to remain suspended until the results of the decision had been reached, some of our decisions in the community college would be different. This suspension would not apply to any of the other provisions of tenure unless the committee actions resulted in the dismissal of the administrator and the others involved. In short, everyone who is responsible for a decision would be held accountable. Only in education do we expect to govern by consensus. But no one has ever heard of a committee getting fired or resigning to retire at the Ford Foundation or to accept a professorship in higher education at a major university. Persons other than administrators should have input in decisions and governance. But input and advice should stop short of decision unless those who demand the right expose themselves to the consequences.

The college is a system made up of students, faculty members, classified personnel, and administration. Each part of the system is dependent upon every other part. When any one component fails to function effectively or attempts to feed on the system, the system eventually ceases to function. If the janitor refuses to clean the toilets for two days, we have a health hazard. If he refuses for a week, we are back in the Middle Ages. No part of the system is more important than another. Today we find most of the components of the system suspect. Many say that the teachers do not teach, that administrators fail to perform their jobs, that classified people have effected a slowdown, and that students continue to suffer as usual. This, perhaps, understates the case.

153

Blind Man on a Freeway

In the final analysis, there are no pat solutions to the problems of administration in the community college. Most of us do not even know what questions to ask. I have not, in these pages, given the blind man sight; perhaps I have offered him insight. If not, let us at least get him off the freeway.

Improving Community Relations

A GUIDE

EDUCATIONAL, EMPLOYMENT, AND HOUSING INFORMATION

1. What is the educational level of the persons of voting age within the community college district? Percentage of persons: who did not attend beyond elementary school, who did not attend beyond high school, who attended beyond high school.
2. What is the employment pattern? Percentage of families: unemployed and/or on welfare, self-employed, salaried, living on retirement income, with working mothers.
3. Housing pattern of community college district. Percentage of: owner-occupied property, public housing, renter-occupied (not publicly owned).
4. Campus area. Percentage: residential, commercial, industrial, other (specify: parks, cemeteries, etc.).

VOTING HISTORY

1. Primary election results: date of election, office, candidate, votes received.
2. City/state general election results: date, issue, number registered, votes cast, percentage of registered who voted.
3. Special election results (other than public school tax and bond elections): date, issue, number registered, votes cast, percentage of registered who voted.

SCHOOL-COMMUNITY ORGANIZATIONS

Name of organization, meeting place, time and date, president or leader, address, telephone, occupation, other key persons in the organization, average monthly attendance (estimate), other pertinent information.

RELIGIOUS INSTITUTIONS

1. Name of church, address, telephone, denomination, officials (title and name), average sabbath attendance.
2. Estimated percentage of membership living within the college district.
3. Do church officials attend school functions (never, seldom, frequently)?
4. What activities does the church sponsor or engage in which are of special interest to the college (tutoring programs, athletic programs, etc.)?

NONPUBLIC SCHOOLS

1. Name of school, address, telephone, name of school head, average enrollment per year, operation of school is—————months per calendar year, type of school (community college, university, secondary, other—specify).
2. Board of regents, board of trustees, alumni, and/or patron organization functioning within the school: name of organization, leader.

SERVICE AND FRATERNAL ORGANIZATIONS

1. Local police station: address, telephone, current chief of police, current juvenile officer, current desk sergeant.
2. Local fire station: address, telephone, current station fire chief.
3. City-operated community centers: name, address, telephone, director.
4. Neighborhood youth corps: address, telephone, director.
5. Branch library: address, telephone, head librarian.
6. United Fund (Good Neighbors) Agencies: name, address, director, telephone.
7. Adult education services: type of class(es), meeting place, organizer.
8. Neighborhood English-language newspapers: name, business office address, telephone, editor.
9. Neighborhood foreign-language newspaper: name, business office address, telephone, editor.
10. Neighborhood ethnic-group newspaper: name, business office address, telephone, editor.
11. Scout organizations: (a) Boy Scouts: troop number, meeting place, scoutmaster, address, telephone. (b) Cub Scouts: pack number, meeting place, cubmaster, address, telephone. (c) Girl

Scouts: troop number, meeting place, leader, address, telephone. (d) Brownies: troop number, meeting place, leader, address, telephone.

12. Neighborhood merchant association: name of organization, purpose, president (address, telephone), other key persons in the organization.

13. Neighborhood improvement associations (block units, etc.): name of organization, purpose, recent community activities, president (address and telephone), other key persons in the organization.

14. Other service and fraternal organizations (American Legion, Rotary, labor unions, etc.). Give specific and pertinent information.

15. Community action groups: name of organization, purpose, director or contact person (address, telephone).

16. Useful school information: List the college and community activities which occur on an annual basis (such as Education Day, fun festivals): activity, when held, where held, sponsored by.

Bibliography

"Accountability." *Education Recaps*, 1970, *9*.

ALLPORT, G. *The Nature of Prejudice*. Garden City, N.Y.: Doubleday, 1958.

ALTMAN, R. A., and SNYDER, P. O. *The Minority Student on the Campus: Expectations and Possibilities*. Boulder, Colo.: Western Interstate Commission for Higher Education, 1971.

BAKER, W. "The Financial Aid Office and Minority Students." In R. A. Altman and P. O. Snyder (Eds.), *The Minority Student on the Campus: Expectations and Possibilities*. Boulder, Colo.: Western Interstate Commission for Higher Education, 1971.

BINNING, D. W. "Open Letter on Open Admissions." *College and University Business*, 1970, *48*(53).

BIRENBAUM, W. A. "White Power and American Higher Education." In R. A. Altman and P. O. Snyder (Eds.), *The Minority Student on the Campus: Expectations and Possibilities*. Boulder, Colo.: Western Interstate Commission for Higher Education, 1971.

BLOCKER, C. E., and others. *The Two-Year College: A Social Synthesis*. Englewood Cliffs, N.J.: Prentice-Hall, 1965.

BOLMAN, F. DE W. "The Administrator as Leader and Statesman." In

G. K. Smith (Ed.), *Stress and Campus Response: Current Issues in Higher Education 1968*. San Francisco: Jossey-Bass, 1968.

CAMPBELL, R., and others. *Introduction to Educational Administration*. Boston: Allyn and Bacon, 1971.

Carnegie Commission on Higher Education. *The Open-Door Colleges: Policies for Community Colleges*. New York: McGraw-Hill, 1970.

Chicago City College. *Food for Thought: Discussion Draft for a Master Plan*. Chicago, 1969.

CLARK, K. B. *Dark Ghetto*. New York: Harper and Row, 1965.

CLEAVER, E. *Soul on Ice*. New York: McGraw-Hill, 1967.

COHEN, A. M. *Dateline '79: Heretical Concepts for the Community College*. Beverly Hills, Calif.: Glencoe, 1969.

COHEN, A. M., and BRAWER, F. B. *Focus on Learning: Preparing Teachers for the Two-Year College*, occasional report no. 11, Junior College Leadership Program. Los Angeles: University of California, 1968.

COLEMAN, J. S., and others. *Equality of Educational Opportunity*. Washington, D.C.: Government Printing Office, 1966.

CONANT, J. B. *Slums and Suburbs: A Commentary on Schools in Metropolitan Areas*. New York: McGraw-Hill, 1961.

CONANT, J. B. "Social Dynamite in Our Large Cities." *Crime and Delinquency*, 1962, *8*(2), 103–115.

CROSS, K. P. "Higher Education's Newest Student." *Junior College Journal*, 1968, *39*(9).

DAVIES, D. "The 'Relevance' of Accountability." *The School Administrator*, 1970, *1*.

DELORIA, V., JR. *Custer Died for Your Sins*. New York: Macmillan, 1969.

DE NEVI, D. " 'Retreading' Teachers the Hard Way." *Junior College Journal*, 1970, *40*(7).

Department of Health, Education, and Welfare. *Career Opportunities in Service to the Disadvantaged and Handicapped*. Washington, D.C., 1969.

DEUTSCH, M. P. "The Disadvantaged Child and the Learning Process." In A. H. Passow (Ed.), *Education in Depressed Areas*. New York: Columbia University Press, 1962.

Bibliography

DUNGAN, R. A. "Higher Education: The Effort to Adjust." *Daedalus,* Winter 1970.

EDDY, E. M. *Walk the White Line: A Profile of Urban Education.* Garden City, N.Y.: Doubleday, 1967.

EGERTON, J. *Higher Education for "High-Risk" Students.* Atlanta: Southern Education Reporting System, 1968.

ELAM, S. "The Age of Accountability Dawns in Texarkana." *Phi Delta Kappan,* June 1970.

ENARSON, H. "The Academic Vice-President or Dean." In G. P. Burns (Ed.), *Administrators in Higher Education: Their Functions and Coordination.* New York: Harper and Row, 1962.

EVANS, R. I. *Resistance to Innovation in Higher Education: A Social Psychological Exploration Focused on Television and the Establishment.* San Francisco: Jossey-Bass, 1967.

GARRISON, R. H. *Teaching in a Junior College: A Brief Professional Orientation.* Washington, D.C.: American Association of Junior Colleges, 1968.

GIBSON, D. "Confrontations." In J. F. Ligon (Ed.), *Proceedings of the Thirty-First Annual Pacific Northwest Conference on Higher Education.* Corvallis, Ore.: Oregon State University Press, 1970.

GLEAZER, E. J., JR. *This Is the Community College.* Boston: Houghton Mifflin, 1968.

GORDON, E. "Jensenism: Another Excuse for Failure to Educate." *IRCD Bulletin,* 1969, *15*(4).

GORDON, E. W., and WILKERSON, D. A. *Compensatory Education for the Disadvantaged: Programs and Practices: Preschool Through College.* New York: College Entrance Examination Board, 1966.

GREENE, M. F., and RYAN, O. *The School Children Growing Up in the Slums.* New York: New American Library, 1964.

HARCLEROAD, F. F. "Accountability and Accreditation." Speech to the United Business Schools Association, Honolulu, Hawaii, November 9, 1970.

HAYAKAWA, S. I. "A Needed Call for Better Teaching." *Seattle Times,* November 25, 1970.

HEISS, A. M. *Challenges to Graduate Schools.* San Francisco: Jossey-Bass, 1970.

HENTOFF, N. *Our Children Are Dying.* New York: Viking, 1966.

161

HIGHTOWER, J. B. "Who Are the Culturally Deprived?" *Saturday Review,* 1970, *7*(18), 41.

HORN, F. H. "The Organization of Colleges and Universities." In G. P. Burns (Ed.), *Administrators in Higher Education: Their Functions and Coordination.* New York: Harper and Row, 1962.

HUFFAKER, C. *Nobody Likes a Drunken Indian.* New York: Paperback Library, 1969.

INGRAHAM, M. H., and KING, F. P. *Mirror of Brass: The Compensation and Working Conditions of College and University Administrators.* Madison: University of Wisconsin Press, 1968.

JACOBSON, L., and ROSENTHAL, R. "Self-Fulfilling Prophecies in the Classroom: Teachers' Expectations as Unintended Determinate of Pupils' Intellectual Competence." In M. Deutsch and others (Eds.), *Social Class, Race and Psychological Development.* New York: Holt, Rinehart, and Winston, 1967.

JENNINGS, F. G. "The Two-Year Stretch: Junior Colleges in America." *Change,* 1970, *15.*

JENSEN, A. "How Much Can We Boost IQ and Scholastic Achievement?" *Harvard Educational Review,* 1969, *39.*

KEETON, M., and others. *Shared Authority on Campus: Report on the Campus Governance Program.* Washington, D.C.: American Association for Higher Education, 1971.

KELLEY, W., and WILBUR, L. *Teaching in the Community Junior College.* New York: Appleton-Century-Crofts, 1970.

KERNER, O., and others. *Report of the National Advisory Commission on Civil Disorders.* Washington, D.C.: Government Printing Office, 1968.

KIERNAN, I. R. "The New Style in College Administration." *Junior College Journal,* 1967, *38,* 22–23.

KITANO, H. L., and MILLER, D. L. *An Assessment of Education Opportunity Programs in California Higher Education.* San Francisco: Scientific Analysis, 1970.

KNOELL, D. M. *Toward Educational Opportunity for All.* New York: State University of New York, 1966.

KNOELL, D. M. "Are Our Colleges Really Accessible to the Poor?" *Junior College Journal,* 1968, *39,* 9–11.

KNOELL, D. M. *People Who Need College: A Report on Students We Have Yet to Serve.* Washington, D.C.: American Association of Junior Colleges, 1970.

Bibliography

KNOELL, D. M., and MEDSKER, L. L. *From Junior to Senior College: A National Study of the Transfer Student.* Washington, D.C.: American Council on Education, 1965.

KOHL, H. *36 Children.* New York: New American Library, 1967.

LESSINGER, L. *Accountability in Education.* Washington, D.C.: National Committee for Support of the Public Schools, 1970a.

LESSINGER, L. "Accountability in Public Education." *Today's Education,* May 1970b.

LESSINGER, L. "Focus on the Learner: Central Concern of Accountability in Education." *Audio-Visual Instruction,* 1970c, *15.*

LESSINGER, L. "How Educational Audits Measure Performance." *Nation's Schools,* 1970d, *85.*

LINOWITZ, S. M., and others. *Campus Tensions: Analysis and Recommendations.* Washington, D.C.: American Council on Education, 1970.

LIVINGSTON, J. C. "Faculty and Administrative Roles in Decision Making." In G. K. Smith (Ed.), *Stress and Campus Response: Current Issues in Higher Education 1968.* San Francisco: Jossey-Bass, 1968.

LLOYD-JONES, E., and ESTRIN, H. A. (Eds.). *The American Student and His College.* Boston: Houghton Mifflin, 1967.

LOMBARDI, J. *Student Activism in Junior College: An Administrator's View.* Washington, D.C.: American Association of Junior Colleges, 1969.

MC GILL, W. J. "Faculty Self Discipline." *San Francisco Chronicle,* July 25, 1971.

MALCOLM X. *The Autobiography of Malcolm X.* New York: Grove, 1964.

MALLAN, J. P. "Some Special Problems of Junior College Faculty." Washington, D.C.: American Association of Junior Colleges, 1968.

MARLAND, S. P., JR. "The Condition of Education in the Nation." *American Education,* 1971, *7*(3).

MEADE, E. J., JR. "Accountability and Governance in Public Education." Address to the annual convention of the National Association of Secondary School Principals, Atlantic City, February 12, 1968.

MEDSKER, L. L. *The Junior College: Progress and Prospect.* New York: McGraw-Hill, 1960.

MEDSKER, L. L., and TILLERY, D. *The Two-Year College in America.* New York: McGraw-Hill, 1970.

MEDSKER, L. L., and TILLERY, D. *Breaking the Access Barriers: A Profile of the Two-Year Colleges.* New York: McGraw-Hill, 1971.

MENSEL, R. F. "Federal Report." *Junior College Journal,* 1971, *41*(8).

MILLER, S. M. "Breaking the Credentials Barrier." Address delivered before the American Ortho-Psychiatric Association, Washington, D.C., March 23, 1967.

MILLETT, J. D. "Accountability in Higher Education." Address to the annual meeting of the Education Commission of the States, Denver, July 9, 1970.

MOORE, W., JR. "The Anatomy of a Developmental Program." In *GT70.* Palatine, Ill.: William Rainey Harper College, 1968a.

MOORE, W., JR. *The General Curriculum: A Program for the Educationally Disadvantaged.* St. Louis: Forest Park Community College, 1968b.

MOORE, W., JR. "Opening the College Gates to the Low Achiever." *Today's Education,* December 1968c.

MOORE, W., JR. "Opportunity for the Disadvantaged." In G. K. Smith (Ed.), *Stress and Campus Response: Current Issues in Higher Education 1968.* San Francisco: Jossey-Bass, 1968d.

MOORE, W., JR., *The Vertical Ghetto: Everyday Life in a Housing Project.* New York: Random House, 1969.

MOORE, W., JR. *Against the Odds: The High-Risk Student in the Community College.* San Francisco: Jossey-Bass, 1970a.

MOORE, W., JR. "Do Community College Teachers Evaluate Their Peers?" Seattle: Seattle Central Community College, 1970b.

MORGAN, G. D. *The Ghetto College Student: A Descriptive Essay on College Youth from the Inner City.* Iowa City: American College Testing Program, 1970.

NEWMAN, F. *Report on Higher Education.* Washington, D.C.: Government Printing Office, 1971.

Newsweek, January 25, 1971.

NICHOLS, R. T. "A Reconsideration of the Ph.D." *The Graduate Journal,* 1967, *12*(2), 325–335.

NUNEZ, R. "The Glaring Reality." In R. A. Altman and P. O. Snyder (Eds.), *The Minority Student on the Campus: Expectations and Possibilities.* Boulder, Colo.: Western Interstate Commission for Higher Education, 1971.

Bibliography

O'DOWD, D. D. "Closing the Gap." In C. B. T. Lee (Ed.), *Improving College Teaching*. Washington, D.C.: American Council on Education, 1967.

PARKINSON, C. N. "On the Making of a College President." *THINK*, September-October 1970, 2.

PEARL, A. "The More We Change, The Worse We Get." *Change*, 1970, *39*.

Phi Delta Kappan, December 1970.

POLLARD, B. L. "Annual Report—General Curriculum." St. Louis: Forest Park Community College, June 1970.

POLLARD, B. L., and others. *Objectives of the Programmed Materials Learning Laboratory*. St. Louis: Forest Park Community College, 1967.

REYNOLDS, R. "Annual Report—Project AHEAD." St. Louis: Forest Park Community College, 1969, 1970.

RHODES, L. "Educational Accountability: Getting It All Together." Speech to a seminar on educational accountability at the Annual Texas Conference for Teacher Education, Dallas, October 1970.

RICHARDSON, R. C., JR. "Needed New Directions in Administration." *Junior College Journal*, March 1970.

RIESSMAN, F. *The Culturally Deprived Child*. New York: Harper and Row, 1962.

ROUECHE, J. E. *Salvage, Redirection, or Custody? Remedial Education in the Junior College*. Washington, D.C.: American Association of Junior Colleges, 1968.

ROUECHE, J. E., and BAKER, G. A. "The Community College President and the Board: Trustees of Accountability." Durham: Regional Education Laboratory for the Carolinas and Virginia, 1970.

ROUECHE, J. E., and others. *Accountability and the Community College: Directions for the 70's*. Washington, D.C.: American Association of Junior Colleges, 1971.

ROWAN, C. Quoted in D. W. Binning, "Open Letter on Open Admissions." *College and University Business*, 1970, *48*(53).

SANFORD, N. *Where Colleges Fail: A Study of the Student as a Person*. San Francisco: Jossey-Bass, 1967.

SCHOONMAKER, A. N. *A Student's Survival Manual: Or How to Get an Education Despite It All*. New York: Harper and Row, 1971.

SCHWARTZ, R. "Accountability." *Nation's Schools*, 1970, *85*.

165

SCRUGGS, M. W. "A Survey on the Number of University Professors in Teacher Training Institutions Who Have Community College Teaching Experience." St. Louis: Forest Park Community College, 1969.

SILBERMAN, C. E. *Crisis in Black and White.* New York: Random House, 1964.

SPENCER, T. "Is Our Integrity Above Reproach?" *Junior College Journal,* 1971, *41*(9).

STEIF, W. F. "Survival and the American Association of Higher Education." *College and University Business,* January 1971.

STEINER, S. *La Raza: The Mexican Americans.* New York: Harper and Row, 1969.

TAYLOR, H. *Students Without Teachers: The Crisis in the University.* New York: McGraw-Hill, 1969.

TAYLOR, H. *How to Change Colleges: Notes on Radical Reform.* New York: Holt, Rinehart, and Winston, 1971.

THORNTON, J. W., JR. *The Community Junior College.* New York: Wiley, 1966.

TRUBOWITZ, S. *A Handbook for Teaching in the Ghetto School.* Chicago: Quadrangle, 1968.

TUNNELL, J. M., JR. "The Proper Burden of Student Leadership." In E. M. Lloyd-Jones and H. A. Estrin (Eds.), *The American Student and His College.* Boston: Houghton Mifflin, 1967.

VAN DEN BERGHE, P. *Academic Gamesmanship.* New York: Abelard-Schuman, 1970.

Washington Post, March 30, 1970.

WILCOX, P. R. "The School and the Community." In *CAP/School Seminar Papers.* Trenton, N.J.: Community Action Training Institute, 1968.

YEGGE, R. "New Legal Relationships Between Institutions and Students." In *The College Campus in 1968,* proceedings of the Seventeenth Legislative Work Conference, Southern Education Board, Austin, July 11–12, 1968.

Index

167

Index

Ethnic composition of community, 150
Ethnic studies, 97
Executive committee of adminstrators, 114

F

Faculty: academic training of, 22, 97, 104; accountability of, 13, 21, 69, 140–141; and administrator, 22, 28, 135; antibigotry workshop for, 122; attitude of toward disadvantaged students, 56, 59, 73–81, 83, 85–87; atypicality of, 100; backgrounds of, 106; bargaining agent of, 63; and board of trustees, 141–142; and change, 2–3, 73, 135–136; characteristics of bargaining groups in, 62; collective bargaining by, 8–9, 16–17, 61–69, 141–146; concern for education by, 61–64, 81; criticism of administration by, 15; demands and grievances of, 15, 24, 61–67, 137; disadvantaged students' criticism of, 75–81; evaluation of, 21, 137–141; excellence of, 145–146; from four-year colleges, 30–31; from high schools, 29; hiring and firing of, 135, 137–138; humanness of, 78, 82; in-service training of, 106; involvement of with students, 78, 82; liberal arts, 30; lives of, 79; militancy among, 24; peer pressures on, 87; performance of, 69, 77, 139–140; Ph.D.s among, 104; as policy makers, 61, 81, 134–138, 141; power of, 9, 15, 19, 28, 75; preparation time for, 64; professionalism of, 13, 19, 62, 81, 141; qualities of good, 82, 147; scholarly work by, 81, 106;
self-serving of, 61, 79; senate of, 85–86; soliciting student support by, 15–19; strikes by, 16, 65, 143–144; versus student needs, 61–67; as teachers, 30, 80–82, 87–88, 95; and using classroom as forum, 15; worship of subject matter by, 80–81, 88
Federal funding, 79, 83
Financial problems, 23–24, 73–74
Foreign-born students, 72
Forest Park Community College, 5
Funds, proposals for, 97

G

GIBSON, D., 57
GLEAZER, E. J., JR., 3
GORDON, E., 76, 96
Government, relations with, 7–8
Graduate school. *See* Training, administrative
Grammar, 90–91
Guidance and counseling degree, 107

H

HARCLEROAD, F. F., 139
HEISS, A. M., 28
Higher education faculty, community college experience of, 5–6
HIGHTOWER, J. B., 76
Hiring: discrimination in, 123–125; faculty role in, 135
Honor students, 94–95
HORN, F. H., 21
Housing patterns, community, 149
HURST, C., 19

I

Impasse advisory committee, 143
In-service training, 106
INGRAHAM, M. H., 2–3, 28
Institute for Junior College Teachers of the Disadvantaged from Urban Ghettos, Title V, 79
Institutional racism, 57

170

Index

Instruction: and curriculum, 90–95; improving, 21–22, 73–74, 82–85; outside influences on, 23

Instrumental function of college, 7

Internship, administrative, 110–111

J

JACOBSON, L., 81, 85
JENNINGS, F. G., 3
Jensenism, 78
Junior colleges, private, 7

K

KEETON, M., 3
KELLEY, W., 3, 15
Kellogg Junior College Leadership Program, W. K., 4, 110, 115
Kerner report, 81
KIERNAN, I. R., 103
KING, F. P., 2–3, 28
KITANO, H. L., 52
Kittrell College, 141
KNOELL, D. M., 10, 70, 75, 96

L

Labor laws, 68
LAYTON, M., 23
Learning problems, 22, 54–55. See also Disadvantaged students
Lecture system, 80
Legislature, 7–8, 118, 148
LESSINGER, L., 139
Librarians, attitudes of, 83, 86
Libraries, 74–75
LIVINGSTON, J. C., 3
LOMBARDI, J., 3, 14, 39

M

MC GILL, W. J., 139
Malcolm X Community College, 19
MALLAN, J. P., 101
Manuals, policies and procedures, 134
MARLAND, S. P., JR., 61, 69
Mathematics, teaching of, 91
MEADE, E. J., JR., 139
MEDSKER, L. L., 3, 10, 88

MENSEL, R. F., 3
Michigan Association of Higher Education, 67
Militants. See Activists, student
MILLER, D. L., 52
MILLETT, J. D., 139
Minorities: activism of, 36, 40, 54, 58–59; arrogance of, 53; attitudes and expectations of, 11; characteristics of, 56; in classroom, 55; college response to, 54; as consultants in antibigotry workshop, 119–121; discrimination against, 52–53; and faculty, 56, 58–59; financial aid for, 59; grievances of, 56–59; hiring of, 51, 57, 123; independence of, 55; learning problems of, 54–55; names of, 59–60; as new constituency, 51–52; propagandizing by, 14; traditional education of, 57; vernacular of, 60-61, 94. See also Disadvantaged students
Minority Affairs Conference, 21
MITCHELL, P. J., 139
Mitchell Junior College, 141
Money, 23–24, 73–74
MOORE, W., JR., 3, 10, 55, 71, 75, 89, 96, 137
Moraine Valley Junior College, 140
MORGAN, G. D., 70, 75, 78, 80, 92
Mothers, unwed, 72
Mount Olive Junior College, 141

N

NASH, G., 59
National Association for the Advancement of Colored People, 122–123
National Education Association, 68
Native Americans, 54, 59. See also Disadvantaged students; Minorities
Negotiation. See Collective bargaining

171

Index

Index

makers, 33; poor, 48, 95; propagandizing by, 13–14; special problems of, 4; transfer, 14; women, 47–50. *See also* Disadvantaged students; Minorities

T

TAFT, R. A., 139
Task-force, administrative, 115
TAYLOR, H., 2–3
TAYLOR, M., 105
Teaching: of disadvantaged students, 94–95; effective, 82, 87–88; evaluation of, 137; of math, 90–91; poor, 78, 80, 95; of reading, 90–92; remedial, 90–94; training for, 106, 111; of writing, 90–91. *See also* Faculty
Tenure, 153
THORNTON, J. W., JR., 10
Training, administrative, 4–7, 29, 31–32; academic courses in, 99, 101, 109–110; by community college, 105–106, 111–112; culture study in, 110; curriculum for, 5–6, 101; developing realistic program for, 107–110; exchange program in, 114; internship in, 110–111; model for, 107, 113; of nonwhites, 112; reasons for bad, 100–101; residency experience in, 112–113; responsibility of community college to define needs of, 106; by task force, 115; by university, 5–6, 101–107; by visiting lecturers, 114
Transfer students, 14

TUNNELL, J. M., JR., 15
Tutoring, 7, 56
Tyler Community College, John, 140

U

Unionization, faculty, 8–9, 16–17, 61–69. *See also* Collective bargaining
University: academic snobbery in, 101; as administrator trainer, 101–103, 106; attitude toward disadvantaged students of, 104; character of, 102; as model, 14, 30–31; racism in, 102; relations of with community college, 102–104; as teacher trainer, 104, 106

V

VAN DEN BERGHE, P., 7
Veterans, 72
Violence, 43–47
Vocational and technical program, 16, 88–89, 137
Voting record, community, 151

W

Watts writing workshops, 91
Westbrook College teacher institutes, 106
WILBUR, L., 3, 15
WILCOX, P. R., 14
WILKERSON, D. A., 96
Women's Liberation Movement, 47–50
Writing, teaching of, 90–91

Y

YEGGE, R., 3